PRACTICE TEST I:

1) The company "Sanfy" employs a team of customer service agents to provide telephone and email support to the customers.

The company develops a webchat bot called "Andrew" to provide automated answers to common customer queries.

Which business benefit should the company expect as a result of creating the webchat bot solution" Andrew"?

A. increased sales

B. a reduced workload for the customer service agents (CSA)

C. improved product reliability

2) For a machine learning (ML) progress, how should you split the data for training and evaluation?

A. Use the features for training and the labels for evaluation.

B. Randomly split the data into rows for evaluation and rows for training.

C. Use the labels for training and the features for evaluation.

D. Randomly split the data into columns for training and columns for evaluation.

3) HOTSPOT

You are developing a model to predict events by using classification.
You have a confusion matrix for the model scored on test data as shown in the following exhibit.

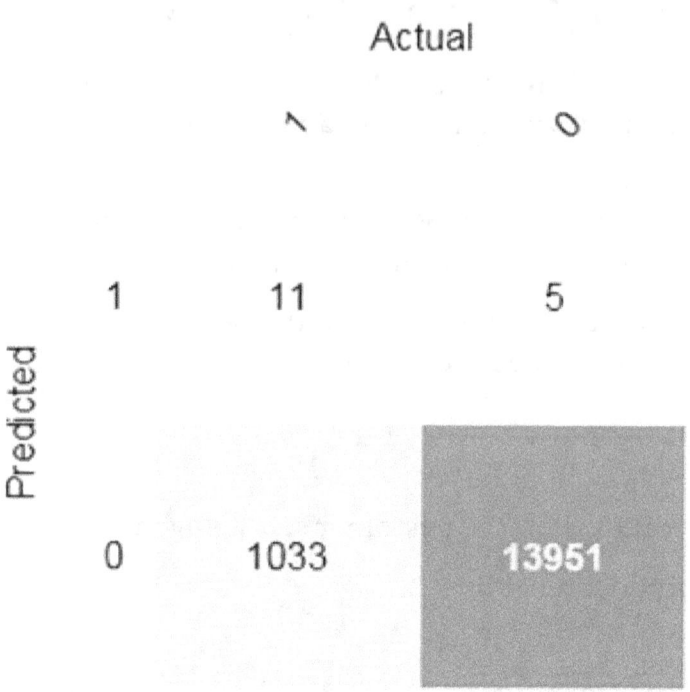

Choose the answer choice that completes each statement based on the information presented in the graphic.

Hot Area:

Answer Area

There are [answer choice] correctly predicted positives.

5
11
1,033
13,951

There are [answer choice] false negatives.

5
11
1,033
13,951

4) You build a machine learning model by using the automated machine learning user interface (UI).

You need to ensure that the model meets the Microsoft transparency principle for responsible AI.

What should you do?

A. Set Validation type to Auto.

B. Enable Explain best model.

C. Set Primary metric to accuracy.

D. Set Max concurrent iterations to 0.

5) HOTSPOT

For each of the following statements, choose Yes if the statement is true. Otherwise, select No.

Hot Area:

Statements:

1) Forecasting housing prices based on historical data is an example of anomaly detection.

2) Identifying suspicious sign-ins by looking for deviations from usual patterns is an example of anomaly detection.

3) Predicting whether a patient will develop diabetes based on the patient's medical history is an example of anomaly detection.

6) HOTSPOT

To complete the sentence, select the appropriate option in the answer area.
Hot Area:

Answer Area

The handling of unusual or missing values provided to an AI system is a consideration for the Microsoft [▼] principle for responsible AI.

- inclusiveness
- privacy and security
- reliability and safety
- transparency

7) DRAG DROP

Match the types of AI workloads to the appropriate scenarios.

To answer, choose the appropriate workload type from the workload's type to its scenario. Each workload type may be used once, more than once, or not at all.
NOTE: Each correct selection is worth one point.

Select and Place:

Workloads Types

| Anomaly detection |
| Computer vision |
| Conversational AI |
| Knowledge mining |
| Natural language processing |

Answer Area

Workload Type	An automated chat to answer questions about refunds and exchange
Workload Type	Determining whether a photo contains a person
Workload Type	Determining whether a review is positive or negative

8) You are designing an AI system that empowers everyone, including people who have hearing, visual, and other impairments.

This is an example of which Microsoft guiding principle for responsible AI?

A. fairness

B. inclusiveness

C. reliability and safety

D. accountability

9) DRAG DROP

Match the Microsoft guiding principles for responsible AI to the appropriate descriptions.

To answer, choose the appropriate principle from the column on the left to its description on the right. Each principle may be used once, more than once, or not at all.

Select and Place:

Principles

| Accountability |

| Fairness |

| Inclusiveness |

| Privacy and security |

| Reliability and safety |

AI-900: Microsoft Azure AI Fundamentals Exam Preparation

New Edition 2025

Achieve success in your **Microsoft AI-900 Azure AI Fundamentals Exam** on the **first try** with our **new** and **exclusive** preparation **book**.

This **Exclusive Book is a preparation** for students who want **to Successfully pass the AI-900: Microsoft Azure AI Fundamentals exam on the first Try!**

Here we've brought **Top new and recurrent Exam Practice Questions for Microsoft AI-900 Azure AI Fundamentals exam** so that you can prepare well for this exam.

This Exclusive **book is** aligned with the **Microsoft AI-900 Exam** Review Manual **2025 edition** and **covers all the exam's topics** that a **Microsoft AI-900** candidate needs to understand in order to **pass the exam successfully.**

The **book practice tests** contain exclusive, **up-to-date content that is designed to match the real exam.**

The Practice tests will **help you gaining** more knowledge and more **confidence** on exam preparation.

You will be able to **self-evaluation** against the **real exam content.**

This book of exclusive **practice tests will test you on questions** asked in the actual Exam.

This exam is intended **for candidates no** matter their prior knowledge or experience.

Skills measured:

Describe AI workloads and considerations (15-20%)

Describe the fundamental principles of machine learning (ML) on Azure (30-35%)

Describe the features of the computer vision (CV) workloads on Azure (15-20%)

Describe the features of the Natural Language Processing (NLP) workloads on Microsoft Azure (15-20%)

Describe features of generative AI workloads on Azure (15-20%)

Who this book is for:

Microsoft Azure AI Fundamentals (AI-900) candidates.

Beginners in Machine Learning (ML)

Welcome!

Answer Area

Principle	Ensure that AI systems operate as they were originally designed, respond to unanticipated conditions, and resist harmful manipulation.
Principle	Implementing processes to ensure that decisions made by AI systems can be overridden by humans.
Principle	Provide consumers with information and controls over the collection, use, and storage of their data.

10) HOTSPOT

To complete the sentence, choose the appropriate option in the answer area.

Hot Area:

When developing an AI system for self-driving cars, the Microsoft for responsible AI should be applied to ensure consistent operation system during unexpected circumstances. 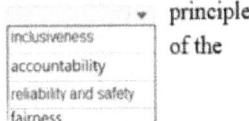 principle of the

- inclusiveness
- accountability
- reliability and safety
- fairness

11) You are building an AI system.

Which task should you include to ensure that the service meets the Microsoft transparency principle for responsible AI?

A. Ensure that all visuals have an associated text that can be read by a screen reader.

B. Enable autoscaling to ensure that a service scale based on demand.

C. Provide documentation to help developers debug code.

D. Ensure that a training dataset is representative of the population.

12) DRAG DROP

Match the types of AI workloads to the appropriate scenarios.

To answer, drag the appropriate workload type from the column on the left to its scenario on the right. Each workload type may be used once, more than once, or not at all.

NOTE: Each correct selection is worth one point.

Select and Place:

Workload Types

- Anomaly detection
- Computer vision
- Machine Learning (Regression)
- Natural language processing

Answer Area

Workload Type	Identify handwritten letters.
Workload Type	Predict the sentiment of a social media post.
Workload Type	Identify a fraudulent credit card payment.
Workload Type	Predict next month's toy sales.

13) Your company is exploring the use of voice recognition technologies in its smart home devices. The company wants to identify any barriers that might unintentionally leave out specific user groups.

This an example of which Microsoft guiding principle for responsible AI?

A. accountability

B. fairness

C. inclusiveness

D. privacy and security

14) What are three Microsoft guiding principles for responsible AI?

Each correct answer presents a complete solution.

A. knowledgeability

B. decisiveness

C. inclusiveness

D. fairness

E. opinionatedness

F. reliability and safety

15) HOTSPOT

To complete the sentence, select the appropriate option in the answer area.

Hot Area:

Answer Area

Returning a bounding box that indicates the location of a vehicle in an image is an example of ▼

| image classification. |
| object detection. |
| optical character recognizer (OCR). |
| semantic segmentation. |

16) HOTSPOT

To complete the sentence, select the appropriate option in the answer area.

Hot Area:

Answer Area

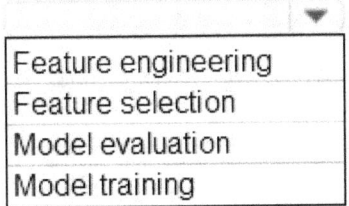 is used to generate additional features.

| Feature engineering |
| Feature selection |
| Model evaluation |
| Model training |

17) You run a charity event that involves posting photos of people wearing sunglasses on Twitter.

You need to ensure that you only retweet photos that meet the following requirements:

∞ Include one or more faces.

∞ Contain at least one person wearing sunglasses.

What should you use to analyze the images?

A. the Verify operation in the Face service

B. the Detect operation in the Face service

C. the Describe Image operation in the Computer Vision service

D. the Analyze Image operation in the Computer Vision service

18) Which metric can you use to evaluate a classification model?

A. true positive rate

B. mean absolute error (MAE)

C. coefficient of determination (R2)

D. root mean squared error (RMSE)

19) Which two components can you drag onto a canvas in Azure Machine Learning designer?

A. dataset

B. compute

C. pipeline

D. module

20) You need to create a training dataset and validation dataset from an existing dataset.

Which module in the Azure Machine Learning designer should you use?

A. Select Columns in Dataset

B. Add Rows

C. Split Data

D. Join Data

21) DRAG DROP

Match the types of machine learning to the appropriate scenarios.

To answer, choose the appropriate machine learning type from the column of learning types to its scenario. Each machine learning type may be used once, more than once, or not at all.

Select and Place:

Learning Types

| Classification |
| Clustering |
| Regression |

Answer Area

Learning Type	Predict how many minutes late a flight will arrive basen on the amount of snowfall at an airpoint.
Learning Type	Segment customers into different groups to support a marketing department.
Learning Type	Predict whether a student will complete a university course.

22) DRAG DROP

Match the machine learning tasks to the appropriate scenarios.

To answer, choose the appropriate task from the column of learning types to its scenario. Each task may be used once, more than once, or not at all.

Select and Place:

Learning Types

| Feature engineering |
| Feature selection |
| Model deployment |
| Model evaluation |
| Model training |

Answer Area

Task	Examining the values of a confusion matrix
Task	Splitting a date into month, day, and year fields
Task	Picking temperature and pressure to train a weather model

23) HOTSPOT

To complete the sentence, select the appropriate option in the answer area.

Hot Area:

Answer Area

Data values that influence the prediction of a model are called

dependant variables.
features.
identifiers.
labels.

24) You have the Predicted vs. True chart shown in the following exhibit.

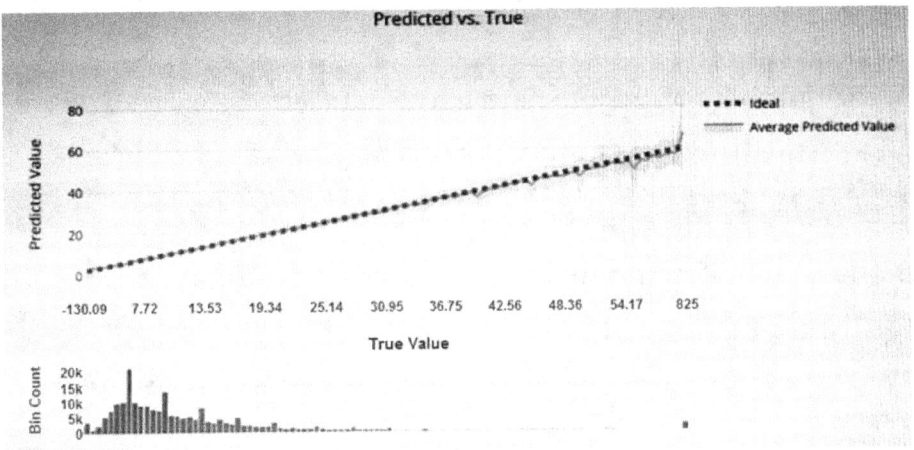

Which type of model is the chart used to evaluate?

A. classification

B. regression

C. clustering

25) Which type of machine learning should you use to predict the number of gift cards that will be sold next month?

A. classification

B. regression

C. clustering

26) You have a dataset that contains information about taxi journeys that occurred during a given period.

You need to train a model to predict the fare of a taxi journey.

What should you use as a feature?

A. the number of taxi journeys in the dataset

B. the trip distance of individual taxi journeys

C. the fare of individual taxi journeys

D. the trip ID of individual taxi journeys

27) You need to predict the sea level in meters for the next 10 years.

Which type of machine learning should you use?

A. classification

B. regression

C. clustering

28) HOTSPOT

For each of the following statements 1 to 4, select Yes if the statement is true. Otherwise, select No.

Hot Area:

Statements:

1) Automated machine learning is the process of automating the time-consuming, iterative tasks of machine learning model development.

2) Automated machine learning can automatically infer the training data from the use case provided.

3) Automated machine learning works by running multiple training iterations that are scored and ranked by the metrics you specify.

4) Automated machine learning enables you to specify a dataset and will automatically understand which label to predict.

29) HOTSPOT

To complete the sentence, select the appropriate option in the answer area.

Hot Area:

Answer Area

A banking system that predicts whether a loan will be repaid is an example of the ⬇ type of machine learning.

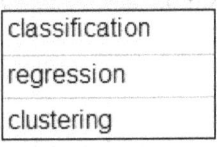

| classification |
| regression |
| clustering |

30) HOTSPOT

For each of the following statements 1 to 3, choose Yes if the statement is true. Otherwise, choose No.

Hot Area:

Statements:

1) Labelling is the process of tagging training data with known values.

2) You should evaluate a model by using the same data used to train the model.

3) Accuracy is always the primary metric used to measure a model's performance.

31) Which service should you use to extract text, key/value pairs, and table data automatically from scanned documents?

A. Form Recognizer

B. Text Analytics

C. Ink Recognizer

D. Custom Vision

32) HOTSPOT

To complete the sentence, choose the appropriate option in the answer area.
Hot Area:

Answer Area

The ability to extract subtotals and totals from a receipt is a capability of the [▼] service.

- Custom Vision
- Form Recognizer
- Ink Recognizer
- Text Analytics

33) You use Azure Machine Learning designer to publish an inference pipeline. Which two parameters should you use to consume the pipeline?

A. the model's name

B. the training endpoint

C. the authentication key

D. the REST endpoint

34) HOTSPOT

To complete the sentence, choose the appropriate option in the answer area.
Hot Area:

Answer Area

From Azure Machine Learning designer, to deploy a real-time inference pipeline as a service for others to consume, you must deploy the model to

a local web service.
Azure Container Instances.
Azure Kubernetes Service (AKS).
Azure Machine Learning compute.

35) HOTSPOT

To complete the sentence, select the appropriate option in the answer area.
Hot Area:

Answer Area

Predicting how many hours of overtime a delivery person will work based on the number of order received is an example of [dropdown]

- classification.
- clustering.
- regression.

36) HOTSPOT

For each of the following statements 1 to 3, choose Yes if the statement is true. Otherwise, choose No.

Hot Area:

Statements:

1) Azure Machine Learning designer provides a drag-and-drop visual canvas to build, test, and deploy machine learning models.

2) Azure Machine Learning designer enables you to save your progress as a pipeline draft.

3) Azure Machine Learning designer enables you to include custom JavaScript functions.

37) HOTSPOT

You have the following dataset.

Household Income	Postal Code	House Price Category
20,000	55555	Low
23,000	20541	Middle
80,000	87960	High

You plan to use the dataset to train a model that will predict the house price categories of houses.

What are Household Income and House Price Category?

To answer, choose the appropriate option in the answer area.

Answer Area

Household Income: [dropdown]
- A feature
- A label

House Price Category: [dropdown]
- A feature
- A label

38) HOTSPOT

To complete the sentence, choose the appropriate option in the answer area.

Hot Area:

Answer Area

Azure Machine Learning designer lets you create machine learning models by [dropdown]
- adding and connecting modules on a visual canvas.
- automatically performing common data preparation tasks.
- automatically selecting an algorithm to build the most accurate model.
- using a code-first notebook experience.

39) HOTSPOT

For each of the following statements 1 to 3, choose Yes if the statement is true. Otherwise, choose No.

Hot Area:

Statements:

1) Automated machine learning provides you with the ability to include custom Python scripts in a training pipeline.

2) Automated machine learning implements machine learning solutions without the need for programming experience.

3) Automated machine learning provides you with the ability to visually connect datasets and modules on an interactive canvas.

40) A medical research project uses a large anonymized dataset of brain scan images that are categorized into predefined brain hemorrhage types.

You need to use machine learning to support early detection of the different brain hemorrhage types in the images before the images are reviewed by a person.

This is an example of which type of machine learning?

A. clustering

B. regression

C. classification

41) When training a model, why should you randomly split the rows into separate subsets?

A. to train the model twice to attain better accuracy

B. to train multiple models simultaneously to attain better performance

C. to test the model by using data that was not used to train the model.

42) Which AI service can be integrated into chat applications to produce text-based content?

A. Azure AI Language

B. Azure AI Metrics Advisor

C. Azure AI Vision

D. Azure OpenAI

43) You need to predict the income range of a given customer by using the following dataset.

First Name	Last Name	Age	Education Level	Income Range
Orlando	Gee	45	University	25,000-50,000
Keith	Harris	36	High school	25,000-50,000
Donna	Carreras	52	University	50,000-75,000
Janet	Gates	21	University	75,000-100,000
Lucy	Harrington	68	High school	50,000-75,000

Which two fields should you use as features?

A. Education Level

B. Last Name

C. Age

D. Income Range

E. First Name

44) You are building a tool that will process your company's product images and identify the products of competitors.

The solution will use a custom model.

Which Azure Cognitive Services service should you use?

A. Custom Vision

B. Form Recognizer

C. Face

D. Computer Vision

45) DRAG DROP

Match the facial recognition tasks to the appropriate questions.

To answer, choose the appropriate task from the column on the left to its question on the right.

Each task may be used once, more than once, or not at all.

Select and Place:

Tasks

grouping

identification

similarity

verification

Answer Area

Task	Do two images of a face belong to the same person?
Task	Does this person look like other people?
Task	Do all the faces belong together?
Task	Who is this person in this group of people?

46) DRAG DROP

Match the types of computer vision workloads to the appropriate scenarios.

To answer, choose the appropriate workload type from the column of the workload's types to its scenario. Each workload type may be used once, more than once, or not at all.

Select and Place:

Workloads Types

| Facial recognition |
| Image classification |
| Object detection |
| Optical character recognition (OCR) |

Answer Area

Workload Type	Identify celebrities in images.
Workload Type	Extract movie title names from movie poster images.
Workload Type	Locate vehicles in images.

47) You need to determine the location of cars in an image so that you can estimate the distance between the cars.

Which type of computer vision should you use?

A. optical character recognition (OCR)

B. object detection

C. image classification

D. face detection

48) HOTSPOT

To complete the sentence, select the appropriate option in the

answer area.
Hot Area:

Answer Area

You can use the [____▼____] service to train an object detection model by using your own images.

| Computer Vision |
| Custom Vision |
| Form Recognizer |
| Video Indexer |

49) You send an image to a Computer Vision API and receive back the annotated image shown in the exhibit.

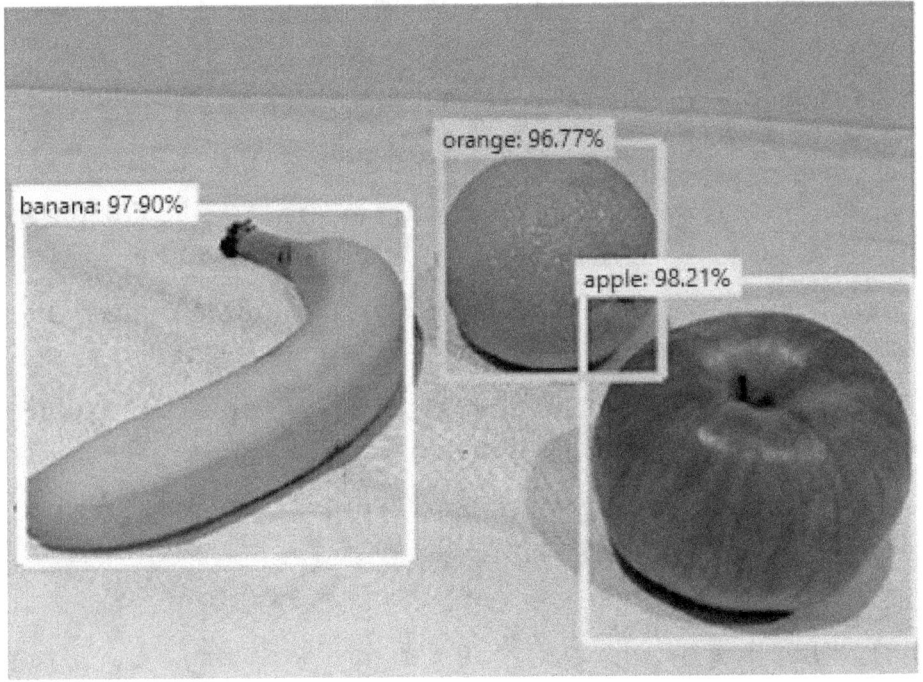

Which type of computer vision was used?

A. object detection

B. semantic segmentation

C. optical character recognition (OCR)

D. image classification

50) What are two tasks that can be performed by using the Computer Vision service?

A. Train a custom image classification model.

B. Detect faces in an image.

C. Recognize handwritten text.

D. Translate the text in an image between languages.

51) What is a use case for classification?

A. predicting how many cups of coffee a person will drink based on how many hours the person slept the previous night.

B. analyzing the contents of images and grouping images that have similar colors

C. predicting whether someone uses a bicycle to travel to work based on the distance from home to work

D. predicting how many minutes it will take someone to run a race based on past race times.

52) What are two tasks that can be performed by using computer vision?

A. Predict stock prices.

B. Detect brands in an image.

C. Detect the color scheme in an image

D. Translate text between languages.

E. Extract key phrases.

53) Your company wants to build a recycling machine for bottles. The recycling machine must automatically identify bottles of the correct shape and reject all other items.

Which type of AI workload should the company use?

A. anomaly detection

B. conversational AI

C. computer vision

D. natural language processing

54) HOTSPOT

For each of the following statements from 1 to 3, choose Yes if the statement is true. Otherwise, choose No.

Hot Area:

Statements:

1) When creating an object detection model in the Custom Vision service, you must choose a classification type of either Multilabel or Multiclass.

2) You can create an object detection model in the Custom Vision service to find the location of content within an image.

3) When creating an object detection model in the Custom Vision service, you can select from a set of predefined domains.

55) In which two scenarios can you use the Form Recognizer service?

A. Extract the invoice number from an invoice.

B. Translate a form from French to English.

C. Find image of product in a catalog.

D. Identify the retailer from a receipt.

56) HOTSPOT

You have a database that contains a list of employees and their photos.

You are tagging new photos of the employees.

For each of the following statements from 1 to 3 choose Yes if the statement is true. Otherwise, choose No.

Hot Area:

Statements:

1) The Face service can be used to group all the employees who have similar facial characteristics.

2) The Face service will be more accurate if you provide more sample photos of each employee from different angles.

3) If an employee is wearing sunglasses, the Face service will always fail to recognize the employee.

57) You need to develop a mobile app for employees to scan and store their expenses while travelling.

Which type of computer vision should you use?

A. semantic segmentation

B. image classification

C. object detection

D. optical character recognition (OCR)

58) HOTSPOT

To complete the sentence, select the appropriate option in the answer area.
Hot Area:

Answer Area

Natural language processing can be used to

classify email messages as work-related or personal.
predict the number of future car rentals.
predict which website visitors will make a transaction.
stop a process in a factory when extremely high temperatures are registered.

59) Which AI service can you use to interpret the meaning of a user input such as Call me back later?

A. Translator Text

B. Text Analytics

C. Speech

D. Language Understanding (LUIS)

60) You are developing a chatbot solution in Azure.

Which service should you use to determine a user's intent?

A. Translator Text

B. QnA Maker

C. Speech

D. Language Understanding (LUIS)

ANSWERS AND EXPLANATIONS:

1) Out of the three options, the most likely benefit for Sanfy from creating the webchat bot "Andrew" is:

B. a reduced workload for the customer service agents (CSA)

Here's why:

Increased sales (A): There's no direct link between a webchat bot and increased sales. While it might improve customer experience, leading to potentially higher customer satisfaction, that doesn't directly translate to sales.

Improved product reliability (C): A webchat bot doesn't address product reliability. It focuses on answering customer questions, not fixing product issues.

Reduced workload for CSAs (B) is a direct benefit of implementing a webchat bot. "Andrew" can handle common customer queries, freeing up CSAs to focus on more complex issues that require human interaction. This can lead to:

Improved agent efficiency.

Reduced wait times for customers with complex problems.

Potentially lower customer service costs.

While webchat bots can offer other benefits, reducing the workload for CSAs is a primary advantage.

2) The best way to split the data for machine learning training and evaluation is:

B. Randomly split the data into rows for evaluation and rows for training.

Here's why the other options are incorrect:

A. Use the features for training and the labels for evaluation: This wouldn't work. The model needs both features (data points) and labels (desired outputs) during training to learn the relationship between them.

C. Use the labels for training and the features for evaluation: Similar to option A, this wouldn't work. The model needs both features and labels during training.

D. Randomly split the data into columns for training and columns for evaluation: Splitting by columns wouldn't work because each row (data point) needs to have both features and labels.

Randomly splitting the data into rows ensures the model is trained and evaluated on a representative sample of the entire dataset. This helps prevent overfitting and allows for a more accurate assessment of the model's performance.

You split rows not columns:

https://docs.microsoft.com/en-us/azure/machine-learning/studio-module-reference/split-data#how-to-configure-split-data

3) Correct Answer:

Answer Area

There are [answer choice] correctly predicted positives.

5
11
1,033
13,951

There are [answer choice] false negatives.

5
11
1,033
13,951

Box 1: 11 –

	Predicted	
	Positive	Negative
Actual True	TP	FN
Actual False	FP	TN

TP = True Positive.

The class labels in the training set can take on only two possible values, which we usually refer to as positive or negative. The positive and negative instances that a classifier predicts correctly are called true positives (TP) and true negatives (TN), respectively. Similarly, the incorrectly classified instances are called false positives (FP) and false negatives (FN).

Box 2: 1,033 –

FN = False Negative –

The grid used in the question is reversed to the MS documentation. A false negative would imply that a 0 was predicted but 1 was the actual outcome, of which there were 1033 occurrences according to the grid used in the question.

Reference:
https://docs.microsoft.com/en-us/azure/machine-learning/studio/evaluate-model-performance

4) The best option to ensure your machine learning model meets the Microsoft transparency principle for responsible AI using an automated machine learning UI is:

B. Enable Explain best model.

Here's why:

Transparency principle: This principle emphasizes understanding how a model arrives at its decisions.

Explain best model: This feature helps explain the predictions made by the best performing model in the automated run. By enabling this, you gain insights into the factors influencing the model's choices, making it more transparent.

Let's analyze the other options:

A. Set Validation type to Auto: While validation is important, it doesn't directly address model transparency. Auto validation helps assess model performance, but it doesn't explain how the model arrives at those results.

C. Set Primary metric to accuracy: While accuracy is a common metric, it might not be the best for all scenarios. Focusing solely on accuracy might not provide insights into the model's decision-making process.

D. Set Max concurrent iterations to 0: This option limits the number of models explored during training. It doesn't directly contribute to understanding the final model's behavior.

Therefore, enabling "Explain best model" directly addresses the transparency principle by providing explanations for the model's predictions.

Model Explain Ability.

Most businesses run on trust and being able to open the ML black box helps build transparency and trust. In heavily regulated industries like healthcare and banking, it is critical to comply with regulations and best practices. One key aspect of this is understanding the relationship between input variables (features) and model output. Knowing both the magnitude and direction of the impact each feature (feature importance) has on the predicted value helps better understand and explain the model. With model explain ability, we enable you to understand feature importance as part of automated ML runs.

Reference:

https://azure.microsoft.com/en-us/blog/new-automated-machine-learning-capabilities-in-azure-machine-learning-service/

5) Correct Answer:

Answer Area

Statements	Yes	No
Forecasting housing prices based on historical data is an example of anomaly detection.	○	◉
Identifying suspicious sign-ins by looking for deviations from usual patterns is an example of anomaly detection.	◉	○
Predicting whether a patient will develop diabetes based on the patient's medical history is an example of anomaly detection.	○	◉

Here's the breakdown of each statement:

Forecasting housing prices based on historical data is an anomaly detection. - No

Identifying suspicious sign-ins by looking for deviations from usual patterns is an anomaly detection. - Yes

Predicting whether a patient will develop diabetes based on the patient's medical history is an anomaly detection. - No

Explanation:

Anomaly detection focuses on identifying data points that deviate significantly from the expected pattern.

Forecasting housing prices uses historical data to predict future trends, which is a form of regression analysis, not anomaly detection.

Identifying suspicious sign-ins involves looking for deviations from a user's usual login patterns (e.g., location, time of day). This aligns with the concept of anomaly detection.

Predicting patient health risks uses medical history to identify potential future developments, similar to forecasting, not anomaly detection.

In anomaly detection, we're interested in finding the outliers, whereas in forecasting and health risk prediction, we're interested in the expected behavior and deviations from that norm to make predictions about the future.

Anomaly detection encompasses many important tasks in machine learning:
Identifying transactions that are potentially fraudulent.
Learning patterns that indicate that a network intrusion has occurred.
Finding abnormal clusters of patients.
Checking values entered into a system.

Reference:
https://docs.microsoft.com/en-us/azure/machine-learning/studio-module-reference/anomaly-detection

6) Correct Answer:

Answer Area

The handling of unusual or missing values provided to an AI system is a consideration for the Microsoft [_____▼_____] principle for responsible AI.

inclusiveness
privacy and security
reliability and safety
transparency

Reliability and safety:

AI systems need to be reliable and safe in order to be trusted. It is important for a system to perform as it was originally designed and for it to respond safely to new situations. Its inherent resilience should resist intended or unintended manipulation. Rigorous testing and validation should be established for operating conditions to ensure that the system responds safely to edge cases, and A/B testing and champion/challenger methods should be integrated into the evaluation process.

An AI system's performance can degrade over time, so a robust monitoring and model tracking process needs to be established to reactively and proactively measure the model's performance and retrain it, as necessary, to modernize it.

"To build trust, it's critical that AI systems operate reliably, safely, and consistently under normal circumstances and in unexpected conditions. These systems should be able to operate as they were originally designed, respond safely to unanticipated conditions, and resist harmful manipulation. It's also important to be able to verify that these systems are behaving as intended under actual operating conditions. How they behave and the variety of conditions they can handle reliably and safely largely reflects the range of situations and circumstances that developers anticipate during design and testing.

We believe that rigorous testing is essential during system development and deployment to ensure AI systems can respond safely in unanticipated situations and edge cases, don't have unexpected performance failures, and don't evolve in ways that are inconsistent with original expectations"

Reference:
https://docs.microsoft.com/en-us/azure/cloud-adoption-framework/innovate/best-practices/trusted-ai

Answer Area

Conversational AI	An automated chat to answer questions about refunds and exchange
Computer vision	Determining whether a photo contains a person
Natural language processing	Determining whether a review is positive or negative

7)

What is Natural Language Processing?

Natural language processing (NLP) is the area of AI that deals with creating software that understands written and spoken language. NLP enables you to create software that can:

-Analyze text documents to extract key phrases and recognize entities (such as places, dates, or people). ie Text Analytics service

-Perform sentiment analysis to determine how positive or negative the language used in a document is. ie Text Analytics service -Interpret spoken language, and synthesize speech responses. ie Speech service (speech to text and text to speech)

-Automatically translate spoken or written phrases between languages. ie Text service (for text-to-text translation)/Speech service (for speech to text/speech translation) Interpret commands and determine appropriate actions. ie Language Understanding (LUIS) service.

8) The Microsoft guiding principle for responsible AI that aligns with designing an AI system that empowers everyone, including people with disabilities, is:

B. Inclusiveness

Here's why:

Inclusiveness: This principle emphasizes designing AI systems that consider the needs of diverse users, including people with disabilities.

Fairness: While fairness is important, it focuses on non-discrimination based on factors like race or gender. In this case, the focus is broader, encompassing accessibility for people with impairments.

Reliability and safety: This principle ensures the AI system functions correctly and avoids causing harm. While important, it doesn't directly address empowering users with disabilities.

Accountability: This principle focuses on taking responsibility for the development and deployment of AI systems. It doesn't directly relate to inclusivity in design.

By following the inclusiveness principle, you ensure your AI system is accessible and usable by everyone, regardless of their abilities. This can involve features like:

Screen readers for visually impaired users

Closed captions for deaf or hard-of-hearing users

Voice control for users with mobility limitations

Simple and clear interfaces for users with cognitive disabilities

Inclusiveness: At Microsoft, we firmly believe everyone should benefit from intelligent technology, meaning it must incorporate and address a broad range of human needs and experiences. For the 1 billion people with disabilities around the world, AI technologies can be a game-changer.

Reference:

Inclusiveness mandates that AI should consider all human races and experiences, and inclusive design practices can help developers to understand and address potential barriers that could unintentionally exclude people. Where possible, speech-to-text, text-to-speech, and visual recognition technology should be used to empower people with hearing, visual, and other impairments.

https://docs.microsoft.com/en-us/learn/modules/responsible-ai-principles/4-guiding-principles

https://learn.microsoft.com/en-us/azure/cloud-adoption-framework/innovate/best-practices/trusted-ai#inclusiveness

9) Correct Answer:

Principles	Answer Area	
Accountability	Reliability and safety	Ensure that AI systems operate as they were originally designed, respond to unanticipated conditions, and resist harmful manipulation.
Fairness	Accountability	Implementing processes to ensure that decisions made by AI systems can be overridden by humans.
Inclusiveness		
Privacy and security	Privacy and security	Provide consumers with information and controls over the collection, use, and storage of their data.
Reliability and safety		

Box 1: Reliability and safety

To build trust, it's critical that AI systems operate reliably, safely, and consistently under normal circumstances and in unexpected conditions. These systems should be able to operate as they were originally designed, respond safely to unanticipated conditions, and resist harmful manipulation.

Box 2: Accountability

The people who design and deploy AI systems must be accountable for how their systems operate. Organizations should draw upon industry standards to develop accountability norms. These norms can ensure that AI systems are not the final authority on any decision that impacts people's lives and that humans maintain meaningful control over otherwise highly autonomous AI systems.

Box 3: Privacy and security

As AI becomes more prevalent, protecting privacy and securing important personal and business information is becoming more critical and complex. With AI, privacy and data security issues require especially close attention because access to data is essential for AI systems to make accurate and informed predictions and decisions about people. AI systems must comply with privacy laws that require transparency about the collection, use, and storage of data and mandate that consumers have appropriate controls to choose how their data is used.

Reference:

https://docs.microsoft.com/en-us/learn/modules/responsible-ai-principles/4-guiding-principles

10) Reliability and safety: To build trust, it's critical that AI systems operate reliably, safely, and consistently under normal circumstances and in unexpected conditions.

These systems should be able to operate as they were originally designed, respond safely to unanticipated conditions, and resist harmful manipulation.

References:

AI systems need to be reliable and safe in order to be trusted. It's important for a system to perform as it was originally designed and for it to respond safely to new situations. Its inherent resilience should resist intended or unintended manipulation. Rigorous testing and validation should be established for operating conditions to ensure that the system responds safely to edge cases, and A/B testing and champion/challenger methods should be integrated into the evaluation process.

https://docs.microsoft.com/en-us/learn/modules/responsible-ai-principles/4-guiding-principles

https://learn.microsoft.com/en-us/azure/cloud-adoption-framework/innovate/best-practices/trusted-ai#reliability-and-safety

11) Correct answer: C. Provide documentation to help developers debug code.

Here's why:

Transparency principle: While the primary focus is understanding model decisions, transparency can also extend to understanding how the model was built and trained.

Debugging documentation: This documentation can include details about the training data, algorithms used, and potential biases identified during development. By making this information accessible, developers can gain insights into the model's behavior, potentially leading to a more transparent and understandable system.

Reference:

Achieving transparency helps the team to understand the data and algorithms used to train the model, what transformation logic was applied to the data, the final model generated, and its associated assets. This information offers insights about how the model was created, which allows it to be reproduced in a transparent way. Snapshots within Azure Machine Learning workspaces support transparency by recording or retraining all training-related assets and metrics involved in the experiment.

https://learn.microsoft.com/en-us/azure/cloud-adoption-framework/innovate/best-practices/trusted-ai#transparency

https://docs.microsoft.com/en-us/learn/modules/responsible-ai-principles/4-guiding-principles

12) Correct answers are:

Answer Area

Computer vision	Identify handwritten letters.
Natural language processing	Predict the sentiment of a social media post.
Anomaly detection	Identify a fraudulent credit card payment.
Machine Learning (Regression)	Predict next month's toy sales.

Computer vision = identify (object) letters

NLP = sentiment

Anomaly Detection = fraud

Machine Learning (regression) = predict

References:

OCR or Optical Character Recognition is also referred to as text recognition or text extraction. Machine-learning based OCR techniques allow you to extract printed or handwritten text from images, such as posters, street signs and product labels, as well as from documents like articles, reports, forms, and invoices. The text is typically extracted as words, text lines, and paragraphs or text blocks, enabling access to digital version of the scanned text. This eliminates or significantly reduces the need for manual data entry.

https://learn.microsoft.com/en-us/azure/cognitive-services/computer-vision/overview-ocr

Regression is a form of machine learning used to understand the relationships between variables to predict a desired outcome. Regression predicts a numeric label or outcome based on variables, or features. For example, an automobile sales company might use the characteristics of a car (such as engine size, number of seats, mileage, and so on) to predict its likely selling price. In this case, the characteristics of the car are the features, and the selling price is the label.

https://learn.microsoft.com/en-us/training/modules/create-regression-model-azure-machine-learning-designer/2-regression-scenarios

Sentiment analysis and opinion mining are features offered by Azure Cognitive Service for Language, a collection of machine learning and AI algorithms in the cloud for developing intelligent applications that involve written language. These features help you find out what people think of your brand or topic by mining text for clues about positive or negative sentiment, and can associate them with specific aspects of the text.

https://learn.microsoft.com/en-us/azure/cognitive-services/language-service/sentiment-opinion-mining/overview

Anomaly Detector is an AI service with a set of APIs, which enables you to monitor and detect anomalies in your time series data with little machine learning (ML) knowledge, either batch validation or real-time inference.

https://learn.microsoft.com/en-us/azure/cognitive-services/anomaly-detector/overview

13) The Microsoft guiding principle for responsible AI that aligns with identifying barriers for user groups in smart home voice recognition technology is:

C. Inclusiveness

Here's why:

Inclusiveness: This principle emphasizes designing AI systems that consider the needs of diverse users, including people with disabilities, cultural backgrounds, and varying accents. In this scenario, the company is specifically looking to avoid unintentional exclusion through voice recognition technology.

Fairness: While fairness is important, it has a broader focus on non-discrimination based on factors like race or gender. Here, the focus is on inclusivity in design to ensure all user groups can interact with the technology.

Accountability: This principle focuses on taking responsibility for the development and deployment of AI systems. It doesn't directly address identifying barriers for specific user groups.

Privacy and security: While important for any AI system, it's not the main focus here. Privacy and security ensure user data is protected, but inclusivity ensures the design caters to a broad range of users.

By following the inclusiveness principle, your company can proactively identify and address potential barriers in the voice recognition technology. This might involve considering factors like:

Background noise: How will the system handle noisy environments?

Accents: Can the system recognize a variety of accents?

Speech impediments: How will the system handle users with speech difficulties?

Age: Can the system understand both younger and older users' voices?

By considering inclusivity from the outset, you can develop a smart home voice recognition technology that is accessible and user-friendly for everyone.

Fairness is also a bit closer. But the device is limited to home appliance. It is not for larger audience where it could go biased.

14) Out of the listed options, three Microsoft guiding principles for responsible AI are:

C. Inclusiveness (as discussed previously)

D. Fairness (ensuring AI systems treat all people fairly and avoid discrimination)

F. Reliability and Safety (ensuring AI systems function correctly and avoid causing harm)

These principles are core aspects of Microsoft's approach to developing and deploying trustworthy AI.

Here's why the other options are not guiding principles:

A. Knowledgeability: While important for AI development, it's not a specific guiding principle.

B. Decisiveness: This isn't a core principle. AI systems should be designed to consider various factors before making decisions.

E. Opinionatedness: AI systems should be objective and unbiased, not opinionated.

The six guiding principles are:

1. Fairness.
2. Inclusiveness.
3. Transparency.
4. Privacy and Security.

5. Reliability and Safety.

6. Accountability.

Reference:

https://docs.microsoft.com/en-us/learn/modules/responsible-ai-principles/4-guiding-principles

15) Correct Answer:

Answer Area

Returning a bounding box that indicates the location of a vehicle in an image is an example of ▼

image classification.
object detection.
optical character recognizer (OCR).
semantic segmentation.

Reference:

Object detection:

Object detection is similar to tagging, but the API returns the bounding box coordinates (in pixels) for each object found in the image. For example, if an image contains a dog, cat and person, the Detect operation will list those objects with their coordinates in the image. You can use this functionality to process the relationships between the objects in an image. It also lets you determine whether there are multiple instances of the same object in an image.

https://docs.microsoft.com/en-us/azure/cognitive-services/computer-vision/concept-object-detection

16) Correct Answer:

Answer Area

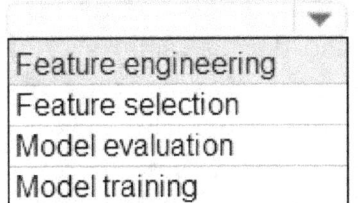 is used to generate additional features.

Feature engineering is applied first to generate additional features, and then feature selection is done to eliminate irrelevant, redundant, or highly correlated features.

Reference:

Although many of the raw data fields can be used directly to train a model, it's often necessary to create additional (engineered) features that provide information that better differentiates patterns in the data. This process is called feature engineering, where the use of domain knowledge of the data is leveraged to create features that, in turn, help machine learning algorithms to learn better.

https://learn.microsoft.com/en-us/azure/machine-learning/how-to-configure-auto-features?view=azureml-api-1#feature-engineering-and-featurization

https://docs.microsoft.com/en-us/azure/architecture/data-science-process/create-features
https://docs.microsoft.com/en-us/azure/machine-learning/team-data-science-process/create-features

17) Correct answer is B. the Detect operation in the Face service.

Explanation: The Detect operation in the Face service is specifically designed to detect faces in images, which aligns with the requirement to include one or more faces in the photos. Additionally, the Face service can also detect facial attributes such as whether a person is wearing sunglasses. This makes it suitable for identifying photos that meet the criteria of including faces and at least one person wearing sunglasses.

Face detect can be requested to detect also glasses attribute

Reference:

"Optionally, face detection can extract a set of face-related attributes, such as head pose, age, emotion, facial hair, and glasses."

https://docs.microsoft.com/en-us/azure/cognitive-services/face/overview

https://docs.microsoft.com/en-us/azure/cognitive-services/face/concepts/face-detection

"Face detect can be requested to detect also glasses attribute"

18) Out of the listed options, the best metric to evaluate a classification model is:

A. True positive rate

Here's why the other options are not ideal for classification models:

B. Mean absolute error (MAE): MAE is commonly used for regression models, which predict continuous values. Classification models predict discrete categories (e.g., spam/not spam, cat/dog). MAE wouldn't accurately reflect the performance of a classification model.

C. Coefficient of determination (R2): R2 is also primarily used for regression models to measure the variance explained by the model. It's not suitable for evaluating classification models.

D. Root mean squared error (RMSE): Similar to MAE, RMSE is a metric for regression models that measures the average magnitude of the errors between predicted and actual values. It's not ideal for classification models.

True positive rate (TPR) is a metric specifically used for evaluating classification models. It represents the proportion of positive cases that were correctly identified by the model. In simpler terms, it tells you what percentage of actual positive examples were classified correctly as positive.

Here are some other commonly used metrics for classification models:

False positive rate (FPR): The proportion of negative cases incorrectly classified as positive.

Precision: The proportion of positive predictions that were actually correct.

Recall: Another term for TPR.

F1-score: A harmonic mean of precision and recall, useful for imbalanced datasets.

The choice of metric depends on the specific context and what aspect of the model's performance is most important. However, TPR (or recall) is a fundamental metric for understanding how well a classification model identifies true positive cases.

What does a good model look like?

An ROC curve that approaches the top left corner with 100% true positive rate and 0% false positive rate will be the best model. A random model would display as a flat line from the bottom left to the top right corner. Worse than random would dip below the y=x line.

Reference:

https://docs.microsoft.com/en-us/azure/machine-learning/how-to-understand-automated-ml#classification

19) In Azure Machine Learning designer, you can drag two of the following components onto a canvas:

A. Dataset

D. Module

Here's why the other options are incorrect:

B. Compute: The compute target specifies the environment where your training pipeline runs. It's typically configured separately and not directly added to the canvas in the designer.

C. Pipeline: A pipeline itself is the collection of steps you create by dragging modules and datasets onto the canvas. It's not a separate draggable component.

In Azure Machine Learning designer, modules represent specific functionalities within your machine learning workflow. Datasets contain the data your modules will work on. By dragging these components onto the canvas and connecting them, you visually build your machine learning pipeline.

Azure Machine Learning designer lets you visually connect datasets and modules on an interactive canvas to create machine learning models.

20) The appropriate module in Azure Machine Learning designer to create a training dataset and validation dataset from an existing dataset is:

C. Split Data

Here's why:

A. Select Columns in Dataset: This module helps choose specific columns from a dataset, not split it into separate datasets for training and validation.

B. Add Rows: This module allows adding new rows to an existing dataset, not splitting it for training and validation.

C. Split Data: This module is specifically designed to split a dataset into multiple datasets based on user-defined ratios. This makes it ideal for creating separate training and validation datasets from your existing data.

D. Join Data: This module combines data from two separate datasets, not splitting a single dataset.

By using the Split Data module, you can specify the desired percentage split between the training and validation datasets. This ensures your model is trained on a representative portion of the data while reserving a separate set for evaluating its performance.

A common way of evaluating a model is to divide the data into a training and test set by using Split Data, and then validate the model on the training data.

Use the Split Data module to divide a dataset into two distinct sets.

The studio currently supports training/validation data splits.

Reference:

https://docs.microsoft.com/en-us/azure/machine-learning/how-to-configure-cross-validation-data-splits

21) Correct Answer:

Learning Types	Answer Area	
Classification	Regression	Predict how many minutes late a flight will arrive basen on the amount of snowfall at an airpoint.
Clustering	Clustering	Segment customers into different groups to support a marketing department.
Regression	Classification	Predict whether a student will complete a university course.

Box 1: Regression

In the most basic sense, regression refers to prediction of a numeric target.

Linear regression attempts to establish a linear relationship between one or more independent variables and a numeric outcome, or dependent variable.

You use this module to define a linear regression method, and then train a model using a labeled dataset. The trained model can then be used to make predictions.

Box 2: Clustering

Clustering, in machine learning, is a method of grouping data points into similar clusters. It is also called segmentation.

Over the years, many clustering algorithms have been

developed. Almost all clustering algorithms use the features of individual items to find similar items. For example, you might apply clustering to find similar people by demographics. You might use clustering with text analysis to group sentences with similar topics or sentiment.

Box 3: Classification

Two-class classification provides the answer to simple two-choice questions such as Yes/No or True/False.

Reference:
https://docs.microsoft.com/en-us/azure/machine-learning/studio-module-reference/linear-regression

22) Correct Answer:

Learning Types	Answer Area	
Feature engineering	Model evaluation	Examining the values of a confusion matrix
Feature selection	Feature engineering	Splitting a date into month, day, and year fields
Model deployment	Feature selection	Picking temperature and pressure to train a weather model
Model evaluation		
Model training		

Box 1: Model evaluation

The Model evaluation module outputs a confusion matrix showing the number of true positives, false negatives, false positives, and true negatives, as well as
ROC, Precision/Recall, and Lift curves.

Box 2: Feature engineering

Feature engineering is the process of using domain knowledge of the data to create features that help ML algorithms learn better. In Azure Machine Learning, scaling and normalization techniques are applied to facilitate feature engineering. Collectively, these techniques and feature engineering are referred to as featurization.

Note: Often, features are created from raw data through a process of feature engineering. For example, a time stamp in itself might not be useful for modeling until the information is transformed into units of days, months, or categories that are relevant to the problem, such as holiday versus working day.

Box 3: Feature selection

In machine learning and statistics, feature selection is the process of selecting a subset of relevant, useful features to use in building an analytical model. Feature selection helps narrow the field of data to the most valuable inputs. Narrowing the field of data helps reduce noise and improve training performance.

Model Evaluation = values

Feature engineering = splitting

Feature selection = picking

Reference:
https://docs.microsoft.com/en-us/azure/machine-learning/studio/evaluate-model-performance https://docs.microsoft.com/en-us/azure/machine-learning/concept-automated-ml

23) Correct Answer:

Answer Area

Data values that influence the prediction of a model are called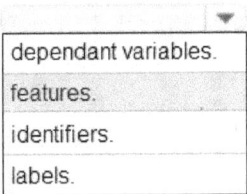

| dependant variables. |
| features. |
| identifiers. |
| labels. |

Here's why:

Dependant variables: These are the variables the model is trying to predict. They are influenced by the features.

Features: These are the data points used by the model to make predictions. They are the independent variables that influence the model's output (the dependent variable).

Identifiers: These are unique values used to distinguish individual data points in a dataset. They don't directly influence the model's predictions.

Labels: These are the target values the model is trying to learn. In some cases, labels can be the same as the dependent variable, but not always.

Reference:
https://www.baeldung.com/cs/feature-vs-label
https://machinelearningmastery.com/discover-feature-engineering-how-to-engineer-features-and-how-to-get-good-at-it/

24) Correct answer: B. regression

What is a Predicted vs. True chart?

Predicted vs. True shows the relationship between a predicted value and its correlating true value for a regression problem.

This graph can be used to measure performance of a model as the closer to the y=x line the predicted values are, the better the accuracy of a predictive model.

Reference:

Regression is a form of machine learning used to understand the relationships between variables to predict a desired outcome. Regression predicts a numeric label or outcome based on variables, or features. For example, an automobile sales company might use the characteristics of a car (such as engine size, number of seats, mileage, and so on) to predict its likely selling price. In this case, the characteristics of the car are the features, and the selling price is the label.

https://learn.microsoft.com/en-us/training/modules/create-regression-model-azure-machine-learning-designer/2-regression-scenarios

https://docs.microsoft.com/en-us/azure/machine-learning/how-to-understand-automated-m

25) The best type of machine learning for predicting the number of gift cards sold next month is:

B. Regression

Here's why:

Classification: This is used for problems where the outcome variable falls into distinct categories (e.g., spam/not spam, cat/dog). Predicting the number of gift cards (a numerical value) doesn't fit this category.

Regression: This is used for predicting continuous numerical values. It's ideal for forecasting sales figures like the number of gift cards sold. The model learns the relationship between historical sales data (features) and the number of gift cards sold (target variable).

Clustering: This groups data points with similar characteristics. It wouldn't directly predict the number of gift cards sold next month.

By using a regression model, you can analyze historical sales data, including factors like time of year, promotions, and economic trends. The model then learns to identify patterns and relationships to predict the number of gift cards likely to be sold in the following month.

In the most basic sense, regression refers to prediction of a numeric target.

Linear regression attempts to establish a linear relationship between one or more independent variables and a numeric outcome, or dependent variable.

You use this module to define a linear regression method, and then train a model using a labeled dataset. The trained model can then be used to make predictions.

Reference:

https://docs.microsoft.com/en-us/azure/machine-learning/studio-module-reference/linear-regression

26) The best feature to use as a predictor for the fare of a taxi journey in this scenario is:

B. the trip distance of individual taxi journeys

Here's why the other options are not ideal features for predicting fare:

A. the number of taxi journeys in the dataset: This represents the overall number of data points, not a characteristic of an individual journey. It wouldn't be helpful in predicting the fare of a specific trip.

C. the fare of individual taxi journeys: This is the target variable you're trying to predict. Including it as a feature would lead to circular reasoning (predicting fare using the fare itself).

D. the trip ID of individual taxi journeys: While the ID might be unique for each trip, it likely doesn't hold any intrinsic value for predicting fare. It's more of an identifier than a feature that captures journey details.

Trip distance is a strong indicator of the fare. Generally, longer trips cost more. By using this feature, the model can learn the relationship between distance and fare, allowing it to predict fares for new journeys based on their distance.

Here are some other potential features that could be helpful for predicting taxi fare:

Pick-up and drop-off locations: These can influence fare due to factors like distance, traffic patterns, and tolls.

Time of day: Fares might be higher during peak hours or on weekends.

Day of the week: Similar to time of day, fares might vary depending on the weekday.

Weather conditions: Traffic congestion due to bad weather could affect fare.

The label is the column you want to predict. The identified Featuresare the inputs you give the model to predict the Label.

Example:

The provided data set contains the following columns:

vendor_id: The ID of the taxi vendor is a feature.

rate_code: The rate type of the taxi trip is a feature.

passenger_count: The number of passengers on the trip is a feature. trip_time_in_secs: The amount of time the trip took. You want to predict the fare of the trip before the trip is completed. At that moment, you don't know how long the trip would take. Thus, the trip time is not a feature and you'll exclude this column from the model. trip_distance: The distance of the trip is a feature. payment_type: The payment method (cash or credit card) is a feature. fare_amount: The total taxi fare paid is the label.

Reference:

Regression is a form of machine learning used to understand the relationships between variables to predict a desired outcome. Regression predicts a numeric label or outcome based on variables, or features. For example, an automobile sales company might use the characteristics of a car (such as engine size, number of seats, mileage, and so on) to predict its likely selling price. In this case, the characteristics of the car are the features, and the selling price is the label.

https://learn.microsoft.com/en-us/training/modules/create-regression-model-azure-machine-learning-designer/2-regression-scenarios

https://docs.microsoft.com/en-us/dotnet/machine-learning/tutorials/predict-prices

27) The best feature to use as a predictor for the fare of a taxi journey in this scenario is:

B. the trip distance of individual taxi journeys

Here's why the other options are not ideal features for predicting fare:

A. the number of taxi journeys in the dataset: This represents the overall number of data points, not a characteristic of an individual journey. It wouldn't be helpful in predicting the fare of a specific trip.

C. the fare of individual taxi journeys: This is the target variable you're trying to predict. Including it as a feature would lead to circular reasoning (predicting fare using the fare itself).

D. the trip ID of individual taxi journeys: While the ID might be unique for each trip, it likely doesn't hold any intrinsic value for predicting fare. It's more of an identifier than a feature that captures journey details.

Trip distance is a strong indicator of the fare. Generally, longer trips cost more. By using this feature, the model can learn the relationship between distance and fare, allowing it to predict fares for new journeys based on their distance.

Here are some other potential features that could be helpful for predicting taxi fare:

Pick-up and drop-off locations: These can influence fare due to factors like distance, traffic patterns, and tolls.

Time of day: Fares might be higher during peak hours or on weekends.

Day of the week: Similar to time of day, fares might vary depending on the weekday.

Weather conditions: Traffic congestion due to bad weather could affect fare.

In the most basic sense, regression refers to prediction of a numeric target.

Linear regression attempts to establish a linear relationship between one or more independent variables and a numeric outcome, or dependent variable.

You use this module to define a linear regression method, and then train a model using a labeled dataset. The trained model can then be used to make predictions.

Reference:

Regression is a form of machine learning used to understand the relationships between variables to predict a desired outcome. Regression predicts a numeric label or outcome based on variables, or features. For example, an automobile sales company might use the characteristics of a car (such as engine size, number of seats, mileage, and so on) to predict its likely selling price. In this case, the characteristics of the car are the features, and the selling price is the label.

https://learn.microsoft.com/en-us/training/modules/create-regression-model-azure-machine-learning-designer/2-regression-scenarios

https://docs.microsoft.com/en-us/azure/machine-learning/studio-module-reference/linear-regression

28) Correct Answer:

Answer Area

Statements	Yes	No
Automated machine learning is the process of automating the time-consuming, iterative tasks of machine learning model development.	O	O
Automated machine learning can automatically infer the training data from the use case provided.	O	O
Automated machine learning works by running multiple training iterations that are scored and ranked by the metrics you specify.	O	O
Automated machine learning enables you to specify a dataset and will automatically understand which label to predict.	O	O

Here's a breakdown of each statement to determine if Automated Machine Learning (AutoML) applies:

Statement 1: Yes

Statement 2: No

Statement 3: Yes

Statement 4: No

Explanation:

Yes: AutoML automates tasks like data preparation, feature selection, model training, and hyperparameter tuning, saving time and effort for data scientists. Automated machine learning, also referred to as automated ML or AutoML, is the process of automating the time consuming, iterative tasks of machine learning model development. It allows data scientists, analysts, and developers to build ML models with high scale, efficiency, and productivity all while sustaining model quality.

No: While AutoML can explore different data sources, it typically requires you to provide the training data. You might need to pre-process or clean the data for AutoML to function effectively.

Yes: AutoML runs multiple training experiments (iterations) with various algorithms and hyperparameter settings. It evaluates each iteration based on your specified metrics and ranks them for your review. During training, Azure Machine Learning creates a number of pipelines in parallel that try different algorithms and parameters for you. The service iterates through ML algorithms paired with feature selections, where each iteration produces a model with a training score. The higher the score, the better the model is considered to "fit" your data. It will stop once it hits the exit criteria defined in the experiment.

No: You need to specify the label (target variable) you want the model to predict. AutoML can't automatically infer this from the use case alone. Apply automated ML when you want Azure Machine Learning to train and tune a model for you using the target metric you specify.
The label is the column you want to predict.

Reference:
https://azure.microsoft.com/en-us/services/machine-learning/automatedml/#features

29) Correct Answer:

Answer Area

A banking system that predicts whether a loan will be repaid is an example of the [classification ▼] type of machine learning.

classification
regression
clustering

Two-class classification provides the answer to simple two-choice questions such as Yes/No or True/False.

Reference:

Classification:

Classification is a form of machine learning that is used to predict which category, or class, an item belongs to. This machine learning technique can be applied to binary and multi-class scenarios. For example, a health clinic might use the characteristics of a patient (such as age, weight, blood pressure, and so on) to predict whether the patient is at risk of diabetes. In this case, the characteristics of the patient are the features, and the label is a binary classification of either 0 or 1, representing non-diabetic or diabetic.

https://learn.microsoft.com/en-us/training/modules/create-classification-model-azure-machine-learning-designer/classification-scenarios

30) Correct Answer:

Answer Area

Statements	Yes	No
Labelling is the process of tagging training data with known values.	O	O
You should evaluate a model by using the same data used to train the model.	O	O
Accuracy is always the primary metric used to measure a model's performance.	O	O

Here's a breakdown of each statement to determine if it's true or false in the context of machine learning:

Statement 1: Yes

Statement 2: No

Statement 3: No

Explanation:

Yes: Labeling is a crucial step in supervised machine learning. It involves adding labels (known target values) to the training data. These labels guide the model in learning the relationship between features and the desired outcome. For instance, if you're training a model to classify images as cats or dogs, each image would be labeled as "cat" or "dog" during this process.

In machine learning, if you have labeled data, that means your data is marked up, or annotated, to show the target, which is the answer you want your machine learning model to predict.

In general, data labeling can refer to tasks that include data tagging, annotation, classification, moderation, transcription, or processing.

No: Evaluating a model on the same data it was trained on can lead to overfitting. Overfitting occurs when a model memorizes the training data too well and performs poorly on unseen data. To assess a model's generalizability, use a separate validation dataset that the model hasn't seen before.

No: Accuracy is a common metric, but it might not always be the best choice. The ideal metric depends on the specific problem you're trying to solve. Here are some considerations:

Classification problems: For imbalanced datasets (where one class has significantly fewer examples), accuracy might be misleading. Metrics like precision, recall, and F1-score can be more informative.

Regression problems: Metrics like mean squared error (MSE) or root mean squared error (RMSE) measure the average magnitude of the errors between predicted and actual values.

Accuracy is simply the proportion of correctly classified instances. It is usually the first metric you look at when evaluating a classifier. However, when the test data is unbalanced (where most of the instances belong to one of the classes), or you are more interested in the performance on either one of the classes, accuracy doesn't really capture the effectiveness of a classifier.

It's important to choose the metrics that best reflect the success criteria for your specific machine learning task.

Reference:
https://www.cloudfactory.com/data-labeling-guide
https://docs.microsoft.com/en-us/azure/machine-learning/studio/evaluate-model-performance

31) The best service for extracting text, key-value pairs, and table data from scanned documents is:

A. Form Recognizer

Here's why:

Form Recognizer is specifically designed for this task. It uses machine learning to understand the structure of documents and extract information accurately.

Text Analytics focuses on analyzing existing text, not extracting it from documents.

Ink Recognizer is for converting handwritten text into digital text, not for understanding the overall document structure.

Custom Vision is used for image recognition, not for document processing.

Accelerate your business processes by automating information extraction. Form Recognizer applies advanced machine learning to accurately extract text, key/ value pairs, and tables from documents. With just a few samples, Form Recognizer tailors its understanding to your documents, both on-premises and in the cloud. Turn forms into usable data at a fraction of the time and cost, so you can focus more time acting on the information rather than compiling it.

Reference:

https://azure.microsoft.com/en-us/services/cognitive-services/form-recognizer/

32) Correct Answer:

Answer Area

The ability to extract subtotals and totals from a receipt is a capability of the [**Form Recognizer**] service.

Dropdown options:
- Custom Vision
- Form Recognizer
- Ink Recognizer
- Text Analytics

Accelerate your business processes by automating information extraction. Form Recognizer applies advanced machine learning to accurately extract text, key/ value pairs, and tables from documents. With just a few samples, Form Recognizer tailors its understanding to your documents, both on-premises and in the cloud. Turn forms into usable data at a fraction of the time and cost, so you can focus more time acting on the information rather than compiling it.

Reference:

https://azure.microsoft.com/en-us/services/cognitive-services/form-recognizer/

33) To consume a published inference pipeline in Azure Machine Learning designer, you'll need two key parameters:

C. The authentication key

D. The REST endpoint

Here's why these are the correct choices:

Authentication Key: This key provides secure access to your published pipeline and ensures only authorized users can interact with it.

REST Endpoint: This is the URL that applications or services use to send requests to your pipeline for predictions. It acts as the entry point for interacting with the published model.

Other options are not required for consumption:

A. The model's name: While the model is part of the pipeline, you don't directly reference it for consumption. The pipeline itself handles the model execution.

B. The training endpoint: This endpoint is used during the training process, not for consuming predictions from the published pipeline.

You can consume a published pipeline in the Published pipelines page. Select a published pipeline and find the REST endpoint of it.

To consume the pipeline, you need:

∽ The REST endpoint for your service

∽ The Primary Key for your service

Reference:

https://docs.microsoft.com/en-in/learn/modules/create-regression-model-azure-machine-learning-designer/deploy-service

34) Correct Answer:

Answer Area

From Azure Machine Learning designer, to deploy a real-time inference pipeline as a service for others to consume, you must deploy the model to ▼

a local web service.
Azure Container Instances.
Azure Kubernetes Service (AKS).
Azure Machine Learning compute.

To perform real-time inferencing, you must deploy a pipeline as a real-time endpoint.
Real-time endpoints must be deployed to an Azure Kubernetes Service cluster.

The real-time endpoint creates an interface between an external application and your scoring model. A call to a real-time endpoint returns prediction results to the application in real-time. To make a call to a real-time endpoint, you pass the API key that was created when you deployed the endpoint. The endpoint is based on REST, a popular architecture choice for web programming projects.

Real-time endpoints must be deployed to an Azure Kubernetes Service cluster.

Reference:
https://docs.microsoft.com/en-us/azure/machine-learning/

concept-designer#deploy

35) Correct Answer:

Answer Area

Predicting how many hours of overtime a delivery person will work based on the number of order received is an example of ▼

| classification. |
| clustering. |
| **regression.** |

In the most basic sense, regression refers to prediction of a numeric target.
Linear regression attempts to establish a linear relationship between one or more independent variables and a numeric outcome, or dependent variable.
You use this module to define a linear regression method, and then train a model using a labeled dataset. The trained model can then be used to make predictions.

Incorrect Answers:

∞ Classification is a machine learning method that uses data to determine the category, type, or class of an item or row of data.

∞ Clustering, in machine learning, is a method of grouping data points into similar clusters. It is also called segmentation.
Over the years, many clustering algorithms have been developed. Almost all clustering algorithms use the features of individual items to find similar items. For example, you might apply clustering to find similar people by demographics. You might use clustering with text analysis to group sentences with similar topics or sentiment.

Note:

Regression = predict time (days, months, year)

Reference:
https://docs.microsoft.com/en-us/azure/machine-learning/algorithm-module-reference/linear-regression https://docs.microsoft.com/en-us/azure/machine-learning/studio-module-reference/machine-learning-initialize-model-clustering

36) Correct Answer:

Statements	Yes	No
Azure Machine Learning designer provides a drag-and-drop visual canvas to build, test, and deploy machine learning models.	O	O
Azure Machine Learning designer enables you to save your progress as a pipeline draft.	O	O
Azure Machine Learning designer enables you to include custom JavaScript functions.	O	O

Box 1: Yes

Azure Machine Learning designer lets you visually connect datasets and modules on an interactive canvas to create machine learning models.

Azure Machine Learning designer is known for its drag-and-drop interface that allows users to build, test, and deploy machine learning models visually. This is beneficial for both beginners and experienced data scientists.

Box 2: Yes

With the designer you can connect the modules to create a pipeline draft.

As you edit a pipeline in the designer, your progress is saved as a pipeline draft.

Azure Machine Learning designer allows you to save your in-progress work as a pipeline draft. This is helpful for iterating on your models and revisiting them later.

Box 3: No

Azure Machine Learning designer currently does not support including custom JavaScript functions within its pipelines. It primarily focuses on a visual approach with pre-built modules and Python/R scripting for customization.

Reference:
https://docs.microsoft.com/en-us/azure/machine-learning/concept-designer

37) Correct Answer:

Answer Area

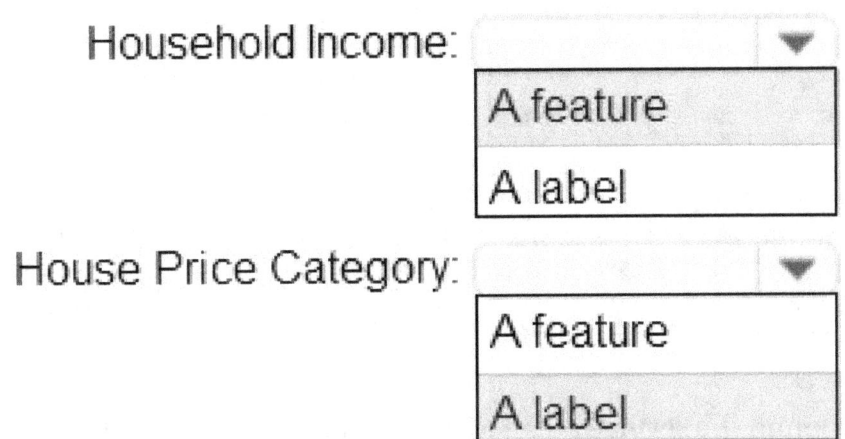

Feature = Input. Label = Output.

Regression is a form of machine learning used to understand the relationships between variables to predict a desired outcome. Regression predicts a numeric label or outcome based on variables, or features. For example, an automobile sales company might use the characteristics of a car (such as engine size, number of seats, mileage, and so on) to predict its likely selling price. In this case, the characteristics of the car are the features, and the selling price is the label.

References:

https://learn.microsoft.com/en-us/training/modules/create-regression-model-azure-machine-learning-designer/2-regression-scenarios
https://docs.microsoft.com/en-us/azure/machine-learning/studio/interpret-model-results

38) Correct Answer:

Answer Area

Azure Machine Learning designer lets you create machine learning models by

adding and connecting modules on a visual canvas.
automatically performing common data preparation tasks.
automatically selecting an algorithm to build the most accurate model.
using a code-first notebook experience.

Although the service is called 'Auto' ML, it is still up to the user to pick the tasks to be automated. Hence, "Adding and connecting modules on visual canvas" is correct.

Reference:
https://docs.microsoft.com/en-us/azure/machine-learning/concept-designer

39) Correct answers are:

1. No, automated machine learning provides you with the ability to include custom Python scripts in a training pipeline.

2. Yes, automated machine learning implements machine learning solutions without the need for programming experience.

3. No, automated machine learning provides you with the ability to visually connect datasets and modules on an interactive canvas.

A) In Automated ML, you cannot insert Python code.

C) in Automated ML, though you can select Data but not modules... No Canvas is used in Auto ML.

There is a DISTINCT difference between Azure Automated Machine Learning that the Machine Learning Designer.

Reference:

No - Automated machine learning only requires you to choose between Python SDK and studio web experience.

Yes - Automated machine learning is a no code solution.

No - This is done in the Azure Machine Learning studio web experience.

https://docs.microsoft.com/en-us/azure/machine-learning/concept-automated-ml

40) The medical research project scenario is an example of:

C. Classification

Here's why:

Clustering groups similar data points together without predefined categories. In this case, the brain scans already have predefined hemorrhage types.

Regression predicts a continuous value based on input data. Hemorrhage types are discrete categories, not continuous values.

Classification categorizes data points into predefined classes. This perfectly fits the scenario where the model needs to classify brain scans into different hemorrhage types based on the image data.

Machine learning classification is ideal for tasks where you want to predict which category a new data point belongs to, considering existing labeled examples. In this case, the model will learn from the labeled images and predict the hemorrhage type for new, unseen images.

The brain hemorrhage types are predefined (labeled), so it's classification.

There are multiple reasons it's classification

- The training data is already tagged as with the correct type of hemorrhage

- Classification can be done for more than two classes (which people seem to not realize based on the comments)

- You do cluster on a group of inputs. For example, the scans of 10 people. You can't cluster a single input. Clearly you get a new scan of a new patient and you want to know what that scan shows, you don't have a group of scans to cluster.

- Clustering gives NO labels. You just get groups and don't know what the label is, but in this question it's very clear they want to know the label that belongs to the new scan -> classification

Reference:

https://docs.microsoft.com/en-us/learn/modules/create-classification-model-azure-machine-learning-designer/introduction

41) The most relevant reason to randomly split the rows into separate subsets when training a model is:

C. To test the model by using data that was not used to train the model.

Here's why:

Splitting the data allows you to evaluate the model's generalizability. If you train the model on all the data, it might simply memorize the patterns in that specific data set and fail to perform well on unseen data.

By using a separate test set, you can assess how well the model performs on data it hasn't encountered during training. This helps ensure the model can learn and apply its knowledge to new situations.

The other options are less likely reasons for splitting data:

A. To train the model twice: While you might train a model multiple times with different hyperparameters, splitting the data is not the primary reason for doing so.

B. To train multiple models simultaneously: Splitting the data can be used for training multiple models on different subsets, but it's not the only approach. You could also train models sequentially on the entire dataset. However, the core purpose of splitting data remains evaluating model performance on unseen data.

This is the famous 70% & 30%

Reference:

https://learn.microsoft.com/en-us/azure/machine-learning/component-reference/split-data?view=azureml-api-2

42) Correct answer: D. Azure OpenAI

Azure OpenAI is the sole service capable of producing text suitable for chat applications to facilitate conversational experiences. Other Azure Cognitive Services are designed for distinct purposes and are not intended for generating text for chat applications.

Azure AI Language offers various functionalities like sentiment analysis and key phrase extraction, but it's not specifically designed for text generation.

Azure AI Metrics Advisor focuses on anomaly detection in time series data, not text generation for chat applications.

Azure AI Vision deals with computer vision tasks like image recognition, not text production.

Azure OpenAI provides access to large language models like GPT-3, which are well-suited for generating different creative text formats, including responses in chat applications. By integrating this service, your chat application can leverage the power of AI to produce human-quality conversational text.

It's important to note that Azure OpenAI is a paid service with usage-based costs.

Reference:

https://learn.microsoft.com/en-us/training/modules/get-started-ai-fundamentals/6-understand-generative-ai

43) Correct answers are:

A. Education Level

C. Age

First Name, Last Name, Age and Education Level are features. Income range is a label (what you want to predict). First Name and Last Name are irrelevant in that they have no bearing on income. Age and Education level are the features you should use.

Regression is a form of machine learning used to understand the relationships between variables to predict a desired outcome. Regression predicts a numeric label or outcome based on variables, or features. For example, an automobile sales company might use the characteristics of a car (such as engine size, number of seats, mileage, and so on) to predict its likely selling price. In this case, the characteristics of the car are the features, and the selling price is the label.

Reference:

https://learn.microsoft.com/en-us/training/modules/create-regression-model-azure-machine-learning-designer/2-regression-scenarios

44) The best Azure Cognitive Services option for building a tool that identifies competitor products in your company's product images using a custom model is:

A. Custom Vision

Here's why:

Custom Vision is specifically designed for creating custom image classification models. It allows you to train your own model on a dataset of labeled images, including those of competitor products.

Form Recognizer focuses on extracting information from forms and documents, not identifying objects in images.

Face is designed for detecting and analyzing human faces, not general object recognition for competitor products.

Computer Vision offers pre-built functionalities for various image analysis tasks, but it wouldn't be ideal for building a custom model focused on competitor product identification.

Custom Vision allows you to:

Train your model on a dataset of competitor product images.

Label the images with the corresponding competitor product names.

Use the trained model to classify new images and identify the competitor products present.

This approach provides a tailored solution for your specific needs of recognizing competitors' products within your company's product images.

Azure Custom Vision is an image recognition service that lets you build, deploy, and improve your own image identifier models. An image identifier applies labels (which represent classifications or objects) to images, according to their detected visual characteristics. Unlike the Computer Vision service, Custom Vision allows you to specify your own labels and train custom models to detect them.

Reference:

https://docs.microsoft.com/en-us/azure/cognitive-services/custom-vision-service/overview

45) Correct Answer:

Tasks	Answer Area	
grouping	verification	Do two images of a face belong to the same person?
identification	similarity	Does this person look like other people?
similarity	grouping	Do all the faces belong together?
verification	identification	Who is this person in this group of people?

verification = same person?

similarity = look like?

grouping = belong together?

identification = who is this person?

Face verification:

The Verify API does an authentication against two detected faces or from one detected face to one person object. Practically, it evaluates whether two faces belong to the same person.

Person identification:

The Identify API is used to identify a detected face against a database of people (facial recognition search). This feature might be useful for automatic image tagging in photo management software. You create the database in advance, and you can edit it over time.

Box 1: verification

Face verification: Check the likelihood that two faces belong to the same person and receive a confidence score.

Box 2: similarity

Box 3: Grouping

Box 4: identification

Face detection: Detect one or more human faces along with attributes such as: age, emotion, pose, smile, and facial hair, including 27 landmarks for each face in the image.

Reference:
https://azure.microsoft.com/en-us/services/cognitive-services/face/#features

https://learn.microsoft.com/en-us/azure/ai-services/computer-vision/overview-identity#face-detection-and-analysis

46) Correct Answer:

Workloads Types	Answer Area	
Facial recognition	Facial recognition	Identify celebrities in images
Image classification	Optical character recognition (OCR)	Extract movie title names from movie poster images
Object detection	Object detection	Locate vehicles in images
Optical character recognition (OCR)		

Box 1: Facial recognition

Face detection that perceives faces and attributes in an image; person identification that matches an individual in your private repository of up to 1 million people; perceived emotion recognition that detects a range of facial expressions like happiness, contempt, neutrality, and fear; and recognition and grouping of similar faces in images.

Box 2: OCR

Box 3: Objection detection

Object detection is similar to tagging, but the API returns the bounding box coordinates (in pixels) for each object found. For example, if an image contains a dog, cat and person, the Detect operation will list those objects together with their coordinates in the image. You can use this functionality to process the relationships between the objects in an image. It also lets you determine whether there are multiple instances of the same tag in an image.

The Detect API applies tags based on the objects or living things identified in the image. There is currently no formal relationship between the tagging taxonomy and the object detection taxonomy. At a conceptual level, the Detect API only finds objects and living things, while the Tag API can also include contextual terms like "indoor", which can't be localized with bounding boxes.

Reference: https://azure.microsoft.com/en-us/services/cognitive-services/face/ https://docs.microsoft.com/en-us/azure/cognitive-services/computer-vision/concept-object-detection

47) The computer vision technique you'll need to locate cars in an image for distance estimation is:

B. Object detection

Here's why:

Optical Character Recognition (OCR) focuses on extracting text from images, which wouldn't be helpful for identifying car locations.

Image Classification classifies an entire image into a single category (e.g., "street scene"). It wouldn't provide specific information about individual objects like cars.

Face detection is designed to identify human faces, not general objects like cars.

Object detection is the ideal choice because it can identify and localize multiple objects (cars) within an image. It provides bounding boxes around the detected cars, allowing you to determine their positions and ultimately estimate the distances between them.

Object detection algorithms can be trained to recognize various object classes, including cars. By applying such a model to your image, you can not only identify the presence of cars but also obtain their locations within the image frame. This information is crucial for calculating the distances between them.

Object detection is similar to tagging, but the API returns the bounding box coordinates (in pixels) for each object found. For example, if an image contains a dog, cat and person, the Detect operation will list those objects together with their coordinates in the image. You can use this functionality to process the relationships between the objects in an image. It also lets you determine whether there are multiple instances of the same tag in an image.

The Detect API applies tags based on the objects or living things identified in the image. There is currently no formal relationship between the tagging taxonomy and the object detection taxonomy. At a conceptual level, the Detect API only finds objects and living things, while the Tag API can also include contextual terms like "indoor", which can't be localized with bounding boxes.

Reference:

https://docs.microsoft.com/en-us/azure/cognitive-services/computer-vision/concept-object-detection

48) Correct Answer:

Answer Area

You can use the [Custom Vision ▼] service to train an object detection model by using your own images.

- Computer Vision
- **Custom Vision**
- Form Recognizer
- Video Indexer

Azure Custom Vision is a cognitive service that lets you build, deploy, and improve your own image classifiers. An image classifier is an AI service that applies labels (which represent classes) to images, according to their visual characteristics. Unlike the Computer Vision service, Custom Vision allows you to specify the labels to apply.

Note: The Custom Vision service uses a machine learning algorithm to apply labels to images. You, the developer, must submit groups of images that feature and lack the characteristics in question. You label the images yourself at the time of submission.

Then the algorithm trains to this data and calculates its own accuracy by testing itself on those same images. Once the algorithm is trained, you can test, retrain, and eventually use it to classify new images according to the needs of your app. You can also export the model itself for offline use.

Incorrect Answers:

Computer Vision:

Azure's Computer Vision service provides developers with access to advanced algorithms that process images and return information based on the visual features you're interested in. For example, Computer Vision can determine whether an image contains adult content, find specific brands or objects, or find human faces.

Reference:
https://docs.microsoft.com/en-us/azure/cognitive-services/custom-vision-service/home

49) Correct answer: A. object detection.

Object detection is similar to tagging, but the API returns the bounding box coordinates (in pixels) for each object found. For example, if an image contains a dog, cat and person, the Detect operation will list those objects together with their coordinates in the image. You can use this functionality to process the relationships between the objects in an image. It also lets you determine whether there are multiple instances of the same tag in an image.

The Detect API applies tags based on the objects or living things identified in the image. There is currently no formal relationship between the tagging taxonomy and the object detection taxonomy. At a conceptual level, the Detect API only finds objects and living things, while the Tag API can also include contextual terms like "indoor", which can't be localized with bounding boxes.

This is indeed object detection, as image classification focuses on identifying a dominant object in an image and assigning it to a category, while object detection focuses on identifying and localizing multiple objects within an image.

References:

https://docs.microsoft.com/en-us/azure/cognitive-services/computer-vision/concept-object-detection

https://learn.microsoft.com/en-us/training/modules/detect-objects-images-custom-vision/1a-what-is-object-detection

50) Correct answers are:

B. Detect faces in an image.

C. Recognize handwritten text.

B: Azure's Computer Vision service provides developers with access to advanced algorithms that process images and return information based on the visual features you're interested in. For example, Computer Vision can determine whether an image contains adult content, find specific brands or objects, or find human faces.

C: Computer Vision includes Optical Character Recognition (OCR) capabilities. You can use the new Read API to extract printed and handwritten text from images and documents.

Microsoft Azure provides multiple cognitive services that you can use to detect and analyze faces, including:

**Computer Vision, which offers face detection and some basic face analysis, such as determining age.

**Video Indexer, which you can use to detect and identify faces in a video.

**Face, which offers pre-built algorithms that can detect, recognize, and analyze faces.

Of these, Face offers the widest range of facial analysis capabilities, so we'll focus on that service in this module.

The ability to extract text from images is handled by the Computer Vision service, which also provides image analysis capabilities.

The Computer Vision service provides two application programming interfaces (APIs) that you can use to read text in images: the OCR API and the Read API.

To be able to submit custom images you need Custom Vision instead of Computer Vision, so it's not A.

Computer Vision Service doesn't allow to translate text, but it allows to identify text, that's why C is correct and not D.

Reference:

https://docs.microsoft.com/en-us/azure/cognitive-services/computer-vision/home

51) correct answer is C.

C. predicting whether someone uses a bicycle to travel to work based on the distance from home to work

Two-class classification provides the answer to simple two-choice questions such as Yes/No or True/False.

Classification is used when you want to predict or classify data into different categories or classes. In this case, predicting whether someone uses a bicycle to travel to work based on the distance from home to work involves categorizing individuals into two classes: those who use a bicycle and those who do not. The distance from home to work is used as a feature to make this prediction.

Incorrect Answers:

A: This is Regression.

B: This is Clustering.

D: This is Regression.

References:

https://docs.microsoft.com/en-us/azure/machine-learning/algorithm-module-reference/linear-regression https://docs.microsoft.com/en-us/azure/machine-learning/studio-module-reference/machine-learning-initialize-model-clustering

52) Computer vision focuses on tasks related to understanding and analyzing visual content. Here are two tasks you can perform using computer vision:

B. Detect brands in an image: Computer vision models can be trained to recognize logos and other brand identifiers within images. This can be helpful for tasks like brand monitoring or product identification in pictures.

C. Detect the color scheme in an image: Computer vision algorithms can analyze the dominant colors present in an image and potentially categorize them into a predefined color scheme (e.g., "monochromatic," "complementary").

Here's why the other options are not ideal fits for computer vision:

A. Predict stock prices: This involves analyzing financial data and economic factors, not visual content. It's a task for financial modeling and machine learning techniques suited for numerical data.

D. Translate text between languages: While computer vision can be used for Optical Character Recognition (OCR) to extract text from images, translation itself is typically handled by Natural Language Processing (NLP) services.

E. Extract key phrases: Similar to translation, this falls under the domain of NLP, which focuses on analyzing and understanding the meaning of textual data.

Reference:

https://docs.microsoft.com/en-us/azure/cognitive-services/computer-vision/overview

53) The ideal AI workload for the bottle recycling machine is:

C. Computer Vision

Here's why:

Anomaly detection focuses on identifying unusual patterns in data, not specifically recognizing objects. While it might be used in later stages to monitor machine performance, it's not ideal for the core task of identifying bottles.

Conversational AI is used for enabling interaction with humans through voice or text. It wouldn't be applicable for the machine's visual recognition of bottles.

Natural Language Processing (NLP) deals with understanding and manipulating human language. It's not relevant for the machine's visual identification task.

Computer Vision is the perfect fit because it excels at analyzing and classifying objects in images. By training a computer vision model on images of acceptable bottles, the machine can identify these bottles in real-time based on their shape and reject any objects that don't match the criteria.

Azure's Computer Vision service gives you access to advanced algorithms that process images and return information based on the visual features you're interested in. For example, Computer Vision can determine whether an image contains adult content, find specific brands or objects, or find human faces.

Anomaly detection is unsupervised learning that detect "deviation" from norm. To correctly identify the "correct" plastic bottle, computer vision should be used.

Reference:

https://docs.microsoft.com/en-us/azure/cognitive-services/computer-vision/overview

54) Correct Answer:

Answer Area

Statements	Yes	No
When creating an object detection model in the Custom Vision service, you must choose a classification type of either **Multilabel** or **Multiclass**.	○	●
You can create an object detection model in the Custom Vision service to find the location of content within an image.	●	○
When creating an object detection model in the Custom Vision service, you can select from a set of predefined domains.	●	○

Here are the answers and explanations:

1. No. When creating an object detection model in the Custom

Vision service, you do not choose a classification type of either Multilabel or Multiclass. Object detection is a separate task from classification. In object detection, the model is trained to identify and locate multiple objects within an image, whereas in classification, the model is trained to assign a single label to an entire image or object.

2. Yes. You can create an object detection model in the Custom Vision service to find the location of content within an image. Object detection models in Custom Vision can identify and locate specific objects within images.

3. Yes. When creating an object detection model in the Custom Vision service, you can select from a set of predefined domains. Predefined domains provide a starting point for training your object detection model by using a preconfigured set of settings and optimizations for specific types of objects, such as general objects, food, or people.

Reference: https://docs.microsoft.com/en-us/azure/cognitive-services/custom-vision-service/get-started-build-detector

55) Form Recognizer is a powerful tool for extracting information from structured documents like forms and invoices. Here are two scenarios where it excels:

A. Extract the invoice number from an invoice: Form Recognizer can be trained to understand the structure of invoices and identify specific fields like the invoice number. It can then extract that information and make it usable within your system.

D. Identify the retailer from a receipt: Similar to invoices, Form Recognizer can be trained to recognize elements on receipts, including the retailer's name. By processing receipts, you can automatically categorize purchases or track spending based on the retailer.

Here's why the other options are not ideal fits for Form Recognizer:

B. Translate a form from French to English: Form Recognizer focuses on extracting information from the document itself, not translating the content. Machine translation services like Azure Translator would be a better choice for this task.

C. Find image of product in a catalog: Form Recognizer deals with structured documents, not searching for images within them. Image recognition services like Azure Cognitive Search with image indexing capabilities might be more suitable for finding product images based on descriptions in a catalog.

Reference:

https://azure.microsoft.com/en-gb/services/cognitive-services/form-recognizer/#features

56) Correct Answer:

Answer Area

Statements	Yes	No
The Face service can be used to group all the employees who have similar facial characteristics.	O	O
The Face service will be more accurate if you provide more sample photos of each employee from different angles.	O	O
If an employee is wearing sunglasses, the Face service will always fail to recognize the employee.	O	O

Here are the answers and explanations:

1. Yes. The Face service can be used to group all the employees who have similar facial characteristics. By analyzing facial

features such as the shape of the face, eyes, nose, and mouth, the Face service can identify similarities between faces and group them accordingly.

2. Yes. The Face service will be more accurate if you provide more sample photos of each employee from different angles. Providing a variety of sample photos helps the Face service to better understand the unique features of each employee's face and improves its ability to recognize them accurately.

3. No. If an employee is wearing sunglasses, the Face service may still be able to recognize the employee depending on the visibility of other facial features. The service is designed to work with a variety of facial characteristics and can often recognize individuals even if they are wearing sunglasses, although wearing sunglasses may reduce the accuracy of recognition.

References:

https://docs.microsoft.com/en-us/azure/cognitive-services/face/overview

https://docs.microsoft.com/en-us/azure/cognitive-services/face/concepts/face-detection

57) The ideal computer vision technique for your expense-scanning mobile app is:

D. Optical Character Recognition (OCR)

Here's why:

Semantic segmentation focuses on pixel-level classification, assigning a category to each pixel in an image. While it could potentially identify receipt regions, it's overkill for this scenario.

Image classification classifies the entire image into a single category (e.g., "receipt"). It wouldn't be helpful for extracting specific data like amounts or vendors from the receipt.

Object detection might identify the receipt itself within the image frame, but it wouldn't extract the text content.

OCR excels at recognizing text within images. This is exactly what you need for the app to scan receipts and automatically extract relevant information like expense details, vendor names, and amounts. By leveraging OCR, the app can convert the visual text data on the receipt into a digital format usable for expense tracking purposes.

Azure's Computer Vision API includes Optical Character Recognition (OCR) capabilities that extract printed or handwritten text from images. You can extract text from images, such as photos of license plates or containers with serial numbers, as well as from documents - invoices, bills, financial reports, articles, and more.

Reference:

https://docs.microsoft.com/en-us/azure/cognitive-services/computer-vision/concept-recognizing-text

58) Correct answer:

Answer Area

Natural language processing can be used to

classify email messages as work-related or personal.
predict the number of future car rentals.
predict which website visitors will make a transaction.
stop a process in a factory when extremely high temperatures are registered.

Natural language processing (NLP) is used for tasks such as

sentiment analysis, topic detection, language detection, key phrase extraction, and document categorization.

Reference:

https://docs.microsoft.com/en-us/azure/architecture/data-guide/technology-choices/natural-language-processing

59) The best AI service to interpret the meaning of a user input like "Call me back later" is:

D. Language Understanding (LUIS)

Here's why:

Translator Text focuses on translating text between languages, not understanding the intent behind user input.

Text Analytics provides functionalities like sentiment analysis and key phrase extraction, but it wouldn't necessarily determine the action implied by the user's statement.

Speech is used for converting spoken language to text. While it might be used in conjunction with LUIS, it wouldn't handle the interpretation itself.

LUIS (Language Understanding) is specifically designed for this purpose. It analyzes user input from text or speech and predicts the overall meaning or intent behind it. In this case, LUIS would recognize that "Call me back later" expresses a request for a callback and potentially extract additional details like preferred contact time if further information is provided in the user input.

Language Understanding (LUIS) is a cloud-based AI service, that applies custom machine-learning intelligence to a user's conversational, natural language text to predict overall meaning, and pull out relevant, detailed information.

Reference:

https://docs.microsoft.com/en-us/azure/cognitive-services/luis/what-is-luis

60) In Azure, the ideal service to determine a user's intent within a chatbot solution is:

D. Language Understanding (LUIS)

Here's why LUIS is the most suitable choice:

Translator Text: This service translates text from one language to another. While it might be used within a chatbot for communication purposes, it wouldn't identify the user's intent behind their message.

QnA Maker: This service excels at finding answers to user questions based on a predefined knowledge base of questions and answers. However, it's not designed for general intent recognition, which involves understanding the broader goal or action the user wants to achieve through their message.

Speech: Speech recognition can be used to convert spoken language to text for processing by LUIS. However, Speech itself doesn't determine the user's intent behind the words.

Language Understanding (LUIS): This service is specifically designed for intent recognition in chatbots and conversational interfaces. It analyzes user text or speech input, extracts key information (entities), and predicts the overall intent behind the user's message. Based on the identified intent, your chatbot can then respond appropriately.

LUIS allows you to define various intents (e.g., "order product," "check order status," "get help") along with example phrases or sentences users might use to express those intents. By training the LUIS model on these examples, it can effectively interpret user messages and determine their conversational goals.

Language Understanding (LUIS) is a cloud-based API service that applies custom machine-learning intelligence to a user's conversational, natural language text to predict overall meaning, and pull out relevant, detailed information.

Design your LUIS model with categories of user intentions called intents. Each intent needs examples of user utterances. Each utterance can provide data that needs to be extracted with machine-learning entities.

Reference:

https://docs.microsoft.com/en-us/azure/cognitive-services/luis/what-is-luis

PRACTICE TEST II

1) You need to make the press releases of your company available in a range of languages. Which service should you use?

A. Translator Text

B. Text Analytics

C. Speech

D. Language Understanding (LUIS)

2) HOTSPOT

For each of the following statements from 1 to 3, choose Yes if the statement is true. Otherwise, select No.

Statements:

1) The Text Analytics service can identify in which language text is written.

2) The Text Analytics service can detect handwritten signatures in a document.

3) The Text Analytics service can identify companies and organizations mentioned in a document.

3) DRAG DROP

Match the types of natural languages processing workloads to the appropriate scenarios.

To answer, match the appropriate workload type to its scenario. Each workload type may be used once, more than once, or not at all.

Select and Place:

Workloads Types

| Entity recognition |

| Key phrase extraction |

| Language modeling |

| Sentiment analysis |

| Natural language processing |

| Translation |

| Speech recognition and speech synthesis |

Answer Area

Workload Type	Extracts persons, locations, and organizations from the text
Workload Type	Evaluates text along a positive-negative scale
Workload Type	Returns text translated to the specified target language

4) HOTSPOT

For each of the following statements from 1 to 3, choose Yes if the statement is true. Otherwise, choose No.

Hot area:

Statements:

1) Monitoring online service reviews for profanities is an example of natural language processing.

2) Identifying brand logos in an image is an example of natural languages processing.

3) Monitoring public news sites for negative mentions of a product is an example of natural language processing.

5) You are developing a natural language processing solution in Azure. The solution will analyze customer reviews and determine how positive or negative each review is.

This is an example of which type of natural language processing workload?

A. language detection

B. sentiment analysis

C. key phrase extraction

D. entity recognition

6) You use natural language processing to process text from a Microsoft news story.
You receive the output shown in the following exhibit.

For weeks now, students and teachers have been settling into the uncharted routine of distance learning. Today I want to thank all of the educators who are connecting classrooms and classmates together in the sudden shift to remote learning. This change requires everyone working together and is unlike anything we've seen in the modern history of education. We've seen countries, school districts and universities move rapidly into remote learning environments with Microsoft Teams being used in 175 countries by 183,000 institutions.

now [DateTime]
students [PersonType]
teachers [PersonType]
distance learning [Skill]
Today [DateTime-Date]
educators [PersonType]
classrooms [Location]
classmates [PersonType]
remote learning [Skill]
history [Skill]
education [Skill]
remote learning [Skill]
Microsoft [Organization]
175 [Quantity-Number]
183,000 [Quantity-Number]

Which type of natural languages processing was performed?

A. entity recognition

B. key phrase extraction

C. sentiment analysis

D. translation

7) DRAG DROP

You plan to apply Text Analytics API features to a technical support ticketing system.

Match the Text Analytics API features to the appropriate natural language processing scenarios.

To answer, match the appropriate feature to its scenario. Each feature may be used once, more than once, or not at all.

Select and Place:

API Features

Entity recognition

Key phrase extraction

Language detection

Sentiment analysis

Answer Area

API Feature	Understand how upset a customer is based on the text contained in the support ticket.
API Feature	Summarize important information from the support ticket.
API Feature	Extract key dates from the support ticket.

8) You are developing a solution that uses the Text Analytics service.

You need to identify the main talking points in a collection of documents.

Which type of natural language processing should you use?

A. entity recognition

B. key phrase extraction

C. sentiment analysis

D. language detection

9) In which two scenarios can you use speech recognition? Each correct answer presents a complete solution.

A. an in-car system that reads text messages aloud

B. providing closed captions for recorded or live videos

C. creating an automated public address system for a train station

D. creating a transcript of a telephone call or meeting.

10) HOTSPOT

To complete the sentence, choose the appropriate option in the answer area.
Hot Area:

Answer Area

While presenting at a conference, your session is transcribed into subtitles for the audience. This is an example of ▼

sentiment analysis.
speech recognition.
speech synthesis.
translation.

11) You need to build an app that will read recipe instructions aloud to support users who have reduced vision.

Which version service should you use?

A. Text Analytics

B. Translator Text

C. Speech

D. Language Understanding (LUIS)

12) HOTSPOT

For each of the following statements from 1 to 3, choose Yes if the statement is true. Otherwise, choose No.

Hot Area:

Statements:

1) You can use the Speech service to transcribe a call to text.

2) You can use the Text Analytics service to extract key entities from a call transcript

3) You can use the Speech service to translate the audio of a call to a different language.

13) Your website has a chatbot to assist customers.

You need to detect when a customer is upset based on what the customer types in the chatbot.

Which type of AI workload should you use?

A. anomaly detection

B. semantic segmentation

C. regression

D. natural language processing

14) You plan to develop a bot that will enable users to query a knowledge base by using natural language processing.

Which two services should you include in the solution?

A. QnA Maker

B. Azure Bot Service

C. Form Recognizer

D. Anomaly Detector

15) You need to provide content for a business chatbot that will help answer simple user queries.

What are three ways to create question and answer text by using QnA Maker? Each correct answer presents a complete solution.

A. Generate the questions and answers from an existing webpage.

B. Use automated machine learning to train a model based on a file that contains the questions.

C. Manually enter the questions and answers.

D. Connect the bot to the Cortana channel and ask questions by using Cortana.

E. Import chit-chat content from a predefined data source.

16) You have a frequently asked questions (FAQ) PDF file.

You need to create a conversational support system based on the FAQ.

Which service should you use?

A. QnA Maker

B. Text Analytics

C. Computer Vision

D. Language Understanding (LUIS)

17) You need to reduce the load on telephone operators by implementing a chatbot to answer simple questions with predefined answers. Which two AI service should you use to achieve the goal? Each correct answer presents part of the solution.

A. Text Analytics

B. QnA Maker

C. Azure Bot Service

D. Translator Text

18) Choose the answer that accurately complete the statement.

[answer choice] Utilize plugins to enable end users to seek assistance with routine tasks from a generative AI model.

A. Copilots

B. Language Understanding solutions

C. Question answering models

D. RESTful API services

19) You have the process shown in the following exhibit.

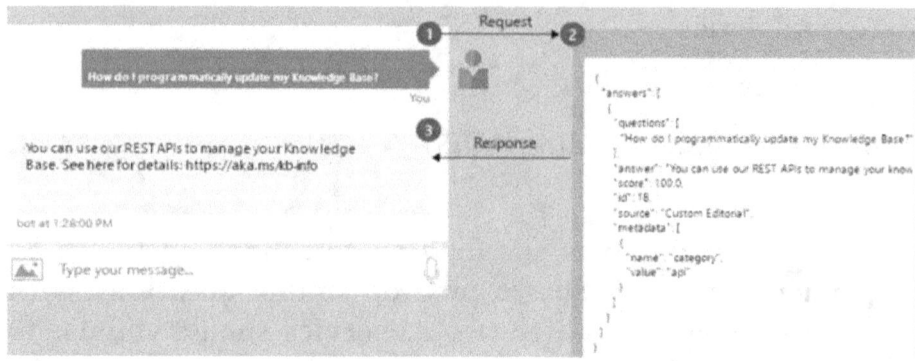

Which type AI solution is shown in the diagram?

A. a sentiment analysis solution

B. a chatbot

C. a machine learning model

D. a computer vision application

20) You need to develop a web-based AI solution for a customer support system. Users must be able to interact with a web app that will guide them to the best resource or answer.

Which service should you use?

A. Custom Vision

B. QnA Maker

C. Translator Text

D. Face

21) Which AI service should you use to create a bot from a frequently asked questions (FAQ) document?

A. QnA Maker

B. Language Understanding (LUIS)

C. Text Analytics

D. Speech

22) HOTSPOT

To complete the sentence, choose the appropriate option in the answer area.
Hot Area:

Answer Area

The interactive answering of questions entered by a user as part of an application is an example of ▼

anomaly detection.
computer vision.
conversational AI.
forecasting.

23) Which scenario is an example of a webchat bot?

A. Determine whether reviews entered on a website for a concert are positive or negative, and then add a thumbs up or thumbs down emoji to the reviews.

B. Translate into English questions entered by customers at a kiosk so that the appropriate person can call the customers back.

C. Accept questions through email, and then route the email messages to the correct person based on the content of the message.

D. From a website interface, answer common questions about scheduled events and ticket purchases for a music festival.

24) HOTSPOT

For each of the following statements from 1 to 3, choose Yes if the statement is true. Otherwise, select No.

Hot Area:

Statements:

1) You can use QnA Maker to query an, Azure SQL database.

2) You should use QnA Maker when you want a knowledge base to provide the same answer to different users who submit similar questions.

3) The QnA Maker service can determine the intent of a user utterance.

25) HOTSPOT

For each of the following statements from 1 to 3, choose Yes if the statement is true. Otherwise, choose No.

Hot Area:

Statements:

1) You can communicate with a bot by using email.

2) You can communicate with a bot by using Microsoft Teams.

3) You can communicate with a bot by using a webchat interface.

26) HOTSPOT

For each of the following statements from 1 to 3, choose Yes if the statement is true. Otherwise, choose No.

Hot Area:

Statements:

1) A restaurant can use a chatbot to empower customers to make reservations by using a website or an app.

2) A restaurant can use a chatbot to answer inquiries about business hours from a webpage.

3) A restaurant can use a chatbot to automate responses to customer reviews on an external website.

27) Which two scenarios are examples of a conversational AI workload?

Each correct answer presents a complete solution.

A. a telephone answering service that has a pre-recorder message

B. a chatbot that provides users with the ability to find answers on a website by themselves

C. telephone voice menus to reduce the load on human resources

D. a service that creates frequently asked questions (FAQ) documents by crawling public websites.

28) HOTSPOT

For each of the following statements from 1 to 3, choose Yes if the statement is true. Otherwise, choose No.

Hot Area:

Statements:

1) Azure Bot Service and Azure Cognitive Services can be integrated.

2) Azure Bot Service engages with customers in a conversational manner.

3) Azure Bot Service can import frequently asked questions (FAQ) to question and answer sets.

29) You have a webchat bot that provides responses from a QnA Maker knowledge base.

You need to ensure that the bot uses user feedback to improve the relevance of the responses over time.

What should you use?

A. key phrase extraction

B. sentiment analysis

C. business logic

D. active learning

30) You are developing a conversational AI solution that will communicate with users through multiple channels including email, Microsoft Teams, and webchat.

Which service should you use?

A. Text Analytics

B. Azure Bot Service

C. Translator

D. Form Recognizer

31) HOTSPOT

For each of the following statements from 1 to 3, choose Yes if the statement is true. Otherwise, choose No.

Hot Area:

Statements:

1) A bot that responds to queries by internal users is an example of a conversational AI workload.

2) An application that displays images relating to an entered search term is an example of a conversational AI workload.

3) A web form used to submit a request to reset a password is an example of a conversational AI workload.

32) Where in the system can you implement content filters to hide prompts and responses for a responsible generative AI solution?

A. metaprompt and grounding

B. model

C. safety system

D. user experience

33) You created an AI solution. Along with solution deployment, you provided information about the solution's possibilities and Limitations.

By providing this information, with what principle for responsible AI did you comply?

A. Fairness

B. Reliability and safety

C. Privacy and security

D. Transparency

E. Inclusiveness

F. Accountability

34) You are working for a car dealership. Your boss asks you to provide him information about how many blue cars he needs to order for the next quarter

You decide to create an ML model and choose an unsupervised machine Learning approach.

Will this help you to achieve your goal?

A. Yes

B. No

35) You are working for a car dealership. Your boss asks you to provide him forecast information: will the new car model be successful or not. The new model has a variety of engine improvements, more comfortable seats, and a sunroof. You compiled the list of data about previous successful models with their characteristics and sales numbers.

What should you do in the pre-processing data stage that would help you to predict the success of the new model?

A. Data selection

B. Training set selection

C. Data for model evaluation selection

D. Feature selection

E. Data classification

36) You created a classification model with four possible classes.

What will be the size of the confusion matrix?

A. 2X2

B. 3X3

C. 4x4

D. 6x6

E. 10X10

37) When you are preparing data for the model training, you have to use your domain knowledge to select the label (or Labels), features. and scale and normalize them.

What is the generic name for the process that includes all the steps mentioned above?

A. Feature selections

B. Data normalization

C. Model training

D. Featurization

E. Missing data handling

38) Choose the answer that accurately complete the statement.

[Answer choice] can provide responses, including text, images, or code, based on natural language input.

A. Computer vision

B. Deep learning

C. Generative AI

D. Machine learning

E. Reinforcement learning

39) Choose the answer that accurately complete the statement.

A. Data grounding

B. Embeddings

C. System messages

D. Tokenization

40) You created a Custom Vision model using the Custom Vision portal.

What information do you need to provide to the developers to use this model?

Please select all that apply

A. Project ID

B. Security Key

C. Model name

D. Prediction key

E. Cognitive Service key

F. Prediction Endpoint

41) Which three sources are suitable for generating questions and answers for a knowledge base? Each correct response provides a comprehensive solution.

A. a webpage

B. an audio file

C. an existing FAQ document

D. an image file

E. manually entered data

42) According to the NIST AI Risk Management Framework, what is the initial stage to contemplate when crafting a responsible generative AI solution?

A. Identify potential harms.

B. Measure the presence of potential harms.

C. Mitigate potential harms.

D. Operate the solution.

43) Which two capabilities exemplify a GPT model? Each correct response provides a comprehensive solution.

A. Create natural language.

B. Detect specific dialects of a language.

C. Generate closed captions in real-time from a video.

D. Synthesize speech.

E. Understand natural language.

44) Which three functionalities exemplify image generation features in a generative AI model? Each correct response provides a comprehensive solution.

A. animation of static images.

B. creating variations of an image.

C. editing an image.

D. extracting RGB values from an image.

E. new image creation.

45) You intend to create an image processing solution that will utilize DALL-E as the generative AI model.

Which capability is NOT supported by the DALL-E model?

A. image description

B. image editing

C. image generation

D. image variations

46) Which generative AI model is employed to create images according to natural language instructions?

A. DALL-E

B. Embeddings

C. GPT-3.5

D. GPT-4

E. Whisper

47) What is the initial step in the statistical analysis of terms in a text within the realm of natural language processing (NLP)?

A. creating a vectorized model

B. counting the occurrences of each word

C. encoding words as numeric features

D. removing stop words

48) What is the confidence score provided by the Azure AI Language Detection service in NLP for an unidentified language?

A. 1

B. -1

C. NaN

D. Unknown

49) Which two features of Azure AI Services can facilitate both text-to-text and speech-to-text translation across multiple

languages? Each correct response contributes to the solution.

A. Conversational Language Understanding

B. key phrase extraction

C. language detection

D. the Speech service

E. the Translator service

50) Which two features of Azure AI Services enable the identification of problems from support question data, along with the recognition of individuals and products mentioned? Each correct response forms part of the solution.

A. Azure AI Bot Service

B. Conversational Language Understanding

C. key phrase extraction

D. named entity recognition

E. Azure AI Speech service

51) Which feature of Azure AI Services for Language enables the analysis of written articles to extract information and concepts, such as individuals and locations, for classification purposes?

A. Azure AI Content Moderator.

B. key phrase extraction.

C. named entity recognition.

D. Personally Identifiable Information (PII) detection.

52) Which three outcomes does the language detection feature of Azure AI Language service return?

A. Bounding box coordinates

B. ISO 6391 Code

C. Language Name

D. Score

E. Wikipedia URL

53) Which functionality of the Azure AI Language service provides links to external websites to clarify terms identified in a text?

A. entity recognition

B. key phrase extraction

C. language detection

D. sentiment analysis

54) What kind of translation does the Azure AI Translator service offer support for?

A. speech-to-speech

B. speech-to-text

C. text-to-speech

D. text-to-text

55) Which Azure resource offers direct access to both Azure AI Translator and Azure AI Speech services using a unified endpoint and authentication key?

A. Azure AI Bot Service

B. Azure AI Services

C. Azure Machine Learning

D. Azure AI Language service

56) You are required to identify numerical values that indicate the likelihood of individuals developing diabetes based on their age and body fat percentage.

Which type of machine learning model should you use?

A. hierarchical clustering

B. linear regression

C. logistic regression

D. multiple linear regression

57) Which machine learning algorithm predicts a numerical label linked to an item based on the features of that item?

A. classification

B. clustering

C. regression

D. unsupervised

58) Which machine learning algorithm determines the best method for dividing a dataset into groups without the need for training and validating label predictions?

A. classification

B. clustering

C. regression

D. supervised

59) A company implements an online marketing campaign on social media platforms to launch a new product. The company aims to utilize machine learning to gauge the sentiment of users on platform X who have posted in response to the campaign.

Which type of machine learning is this?

A. classification

B. clustering

C. data transformation

D. regression

60) A healthcare organization possesses a dataset comprising bone fracture scans categorized by predefined fracture types. The organization seeks to employ machine learning to identify the various types of bone fractures in new scans prior to their review by a medical practitioner.

Which type of machine learning is this?

A. classification

B. clustering

C. featurization

D. regression

ANSWERS AND EXPLANATION:

1) The correct answer is A. Translator.

Translator is a Microsoft Azure service that provides text translation between various languages. It can be used to make written press releases available in a range of languages by translating the content. Text Analytics (option B) is used for extracting insights and sentiment analysis from text. Speech (option C) is used for speech-to-text and text-to-speech conversion. Language Understanding (LUIS) (option D) is used for building natural language understanding into apps, but it's not directly related to translating written content into multiple languages.

Translator is a cloud-based machine translation service you can use to translate text in near real-time through a simple REST API call. The service uses modern neural machine translation technology and offers statistical machine translation technology. Custom Translator is an extension of Translator, which allows you to build neural translation systems.

Reference:
https://docs.microsoft.com/en-us/azure/cognitive-services/translator/

2) Correct Answer:

Answer Area

Statements	Yes	No
The Text Analytics service can identify in which language text is written.	●	○
The Text Analytics service can detect handwritten signatures in a document.	○	●
The Text Analytics service can identify companies and organizations mentioned in a document.	●	○

The Text Analytics API is a cloud-based service that provides advanced natural language processing over raw text, and includes four main functions: sentiment analysis, key phrase extraction, named entity recognition, and language detection.

Box 1: Yes

You can detect which language the input text is written in and report a single language code for every document submitted on the request in a wide range of languages, variants, dialects, and some regional/cultural languages. The language code is paired with a score indicating the strength of the score. The Text Analytics service is specifically designed for analyzing text data and one of its functionalities is language detection. It can identify the language a piece of text is written in and provide a confidence score.

Box 2: No

Text Analytics focuses on analyzing the actual text content, not recognizing visual elements like handwritten signatures. Handwritten text recognition is a separate field called Optical Character Recognition (OCR).

Box 3: Yes

Named Entity Recognition: Identify and categorize entities in your text as people, places, organizations, date/time, quantities, percentages, currencies, and more.

Well-known entities are also recognized and linked to more information on the web. Text Analytics includes a feature called named entity recognition, which can identify and categorize entities like people, locations, and organizations mentioned in the text. This would include identifying companies and organizations.

Reference:
https://docs.microsoft.com/en-us/azure/cognitive-services/text-analytics/overview

3) Correct Answer:

Workloads Types
Entity recognition
Key phrase extraction
Language modeling
Sentiment analysis
Natural language processing
Translation
Speech recognition and speech synthesis

Answer Area	
Entity recognition	Extracts persons, locations, and organizations from the text
Sentiment analysis	Evaluates text along a positive-negative scale
Translation	Returns text translated to the specified target language

Box 1: Entity recognition

Named Entity Recognition (NER) is the ability to identify different entities in text and categorize them into pre-defined classes or types such as: person, location, event, product, and organization.

Box 2: Sentiment analysis

Sentiment Analysis is the process of determining whether a piece of writing is positive, negative or neutral.

Box 3: Translation

Using Microsoft's Translator text API
This versatile API from Microsoft can be used for the following:

Translate text from one language to another.
Transliterate text from one script to another.
Detecting language of the input text.
Find alternate translations to specific text.
Determine the sentence length.

Reference:
https://docs.microsoft.com/en-in/azure/cognitive-services/text-analytics/how-tos/text-analytics-how-to-entity-linking?tabs=version-3-preview

https://azure.microsoft.com/en-us/services/cognitive-services/text-analytics

4) Correct Answer:

Answer Area

Statements	Yes	No
Monitoring online service reviews for profanities is an example of natural language processing.	O	
Identifying brand logos in an image is an example of natural languages processing.		O
Monitoring public news sites for negative mentions of a product is an example of natural language processing.	O	

Box 1: Yes

Content Moderator is part of Microsoft Cognitive Services

allowing businesses to use machine assisted moderation of text, images, and videos that augment human review.

The text moderation capability now includes a new machine-learning based text classification feature which uses a trained model to identify possible abusive, derogatory or discriminatory language such as slang, abbreviated words, offensive, and intentionally misspelled words for review.

Natural Language Processing (NLP) deals with understanding the meaning and intent behind human language. Monitoring online reviews for profanities involves analyzing the text and identifying words or phrases that violate certain guidelines. This is a classic NLP task of sentiment analysis.

Box 2: No

Azure's Computer Vision service gives you access to advanced algorithms that process images and return information based on the visual features you're interested in. For example, Computer Vision can determine whether an image contains adult content, find specific brands or objects, or find human faces. Identifying logos in an image is a computer vision task, not NLP. NLP deals with understanding text data, while computer vision focuses on extracting meaning from visual information like images.

Box 3: Yes

Natural language processing (NLP) is used for tasks such as sentiment analysis, topic detection, language detection, key phrase extraction, and document categorization.

Monitoring news sites for negative mentions of a product involves analyzing the text and understanding the sentiment expressed. NLP techniques can be used to identify negative opinions and keywords related to the product.

Sentiment Analysis is the process of determining whether a piece of writing is positive, negative or neutral.

Reference:
https://azure.microsoft.com/es-es/blog/machine-assisted-text-classification-on-content-moderator-public-preview/

https://docs.microsoft.com/en-us/azure/architecture/data-guide/technology-choices/natural-language-processing

5) The correct answer is:

B. sentiment analysis

Here's why the other options are incorrect:

Language detection: This task involves identifying the language a piece of text is written in. While it might be a preliminary step in processing customer reviews, it's not the core analysis of the sentiment itself.

Key phrase extraction: This task identifies important phrases within the text. While sentiment analysis might utilize key phrases associated with positive or negative emotions, it's focused on the overall sentiment expressed in the review.

Entity recognition: This task focuses on identifying named entities in text, such as people, organizations, locations, etc. While reviews might mention products or brands, the core analysis here is understanding the emotional tone of the review, not identifying specific entities.

Sentiment analysis is the most fitting option as it directly addresses the task of determining the positive or negative nature of customer reviews.

Sentiment Analysis is the process of determining whether a piece of writing is positive, negative or neutral.

Reference:

https://docs.microsoft.com/en-us/azure/architecture/data-guide/technology-choices/natural-language-processing

6) Correct answer: A. entity recognition.

Named Entity Recognition (NER) is the ability to identify different entities in text and categorize them into pre-defined classes or types such as: person, location, event, product, and organization.

In this question, the square brackets indicate the entities such as DateTime, PersonType, Skill.

Extract a broad range of pre-built entities such as people, places, organizations, date/time, numerals and over 100 types of personally identifiable information (PII), including protected health information (PHI), in documents using named entity recognition.

Quickly evaluate and identify the main points in unstructured text. Get a list of relevant phrases that best describe the subject of each record using key phrase extraction. Easily organize information to make sense of important topics and trends.

References:

Entity recognition has category classification, key phrase

extraction does not. Take a look at Key Phrase extraction results:

https://docs.microsoft.com/en-us/azure/cognitive-services/text-analytics/how-tos/text-analytics-how-to-keyword-extraction

With NER results:

https://docs.microsoft.com/en-us/azure/cognitive-services/text-analytics/how-tos/text-analytics-how-to-entity-linking?tabs=version-3-preview

7) Correct Answer:

API Features	Answer Area	
Entity recognition	Sentiment analysis	Understand how upset a customer is based on the text contained in the support ticket.
Key phrase extraction	Key phrase extraction	Summarize important information from the support ticket.
Language detection	Entity recognition	Extract key dates from the support ticket.
Sentiment analysis		

Box1: Sentiment analysis

Sentiment Analysis is the process of determining whether a piece of writing is positive, negative or neutral.

Box 2: Broad entity extraction

Broad entity extraction: Identify important concepts in text, including key
Key phrase extraction/ Broad entity extraction: Identify important concepts in text, including key phrases and named entities such as people, places, and organizations.

Box 3: Entity Recognition

Named Entity Recognition: Identify and categorize entities in your text as people, places, organizations, date/time, quantities, percentages, currencies, and more.
Well-known entities are also recognized and linked to more information on the web.

Reference:
https://docs.microsoft.com/en-us/azure/architecture/data-guide/technology-choices/natural-language-processing

https://azure.microsoft.com/en-us/services/cognitive-services/text-analytics

8) The best type of NLP for identifying main talking points is:

B. key phrase extraction

Here's why the other options are incorrect:

Entity recognition: This identifies specific named entities like people, organizations, locations, etc. While some entities might be related to the main points, it's not focused on summarizing the overall themes.

Sentiment analysis: This determines the emotional tone of the text (positive, negative, neutral). While sentiment can be helpful in understanding the overall message, it doesn't directly address the main talking points.

Language detection: This identifies the language the text is written in. This wouldn't help determine the main points of the documents.

Key phrase extraction focuses on identifying the most important phrases that capture the essence of the text. This aligns perfectly with the goal of summarizing the main talking points in a collection of documents.

Broad entity extraction: Identify important concepts in text, including key.

Key phrase extraction/ Broad entity extraction: Identify important concepts in text, including key phrases and named entities such as people, places, and organizations.

Reference:

https://docs.microsoft.com/en-us/azure/architecture/data-guide/technology-choices/natural-language-processing

9) Correct answers are:

B. Providing closed captions for recorded or live videos.

D. Creating a transcript of a telephone call or meeting.

Explanation:

B. Speech recognition can be used to transcribe spoken words into text, which can then be used for closed captions in videos to make them accessible to people with hearing impairments.

D. Speech recognition can also be used to transcribe telephone calls or meetings, converting the spoken words into a written transcript for documentation or reference purposes.

hint -> Speech Recognition is Speech to Text.

Speech Synthesis is the reverse.

Reference:

https://azure.microsoft.com/en-gb/services/cognitive-services/

speech-to-text/#features

10) Correct Answer:

Answer Area

While presenting at a conference, your session is transcribed into subtitles for the audience. This is an example of ▼

| sentiment analysis. |
| speech recognition. |
| speech synthesis. |
| translation. |

The correct answer is speech recognition.

The image you sent shows a slide from a presentation where the speaker is discussing speech recognition. The text on the slide says:

While presenting at a conference, your session is transcribed into subtitles for the audience. This is an example of speech recognition.

Speech recognition is the process of converting spoken language into text. In the image, the speaker's session is being transcribed into subtitles in real time, which is a common application of speech recognition.

Reference:
https://azure.microsoft.com/en-gb/services/cognitive-services/speech-to-text/#features

11) The best service for this scenario is:

C. Speech

Here's why the other options are not ideal:

A. Text Analytics: This service focuses on analyzing text data, not converting it to speech. While it might be used for preliminary tasks like language detection, it wouldn't help with reading instructions aloud.

B. Translator Text: This service translates text from one language to another. While the recipe instructions might be in a different language, the core functionality needed is converting text to speech, not translation.

D. Language Understanding (LUIS): This service is for understanding the intent behind natural language used in applications. While it might be helpful for future functionalities within the app, it's not directly related to converting recipe instructions to speech.

Speech (Text-to-Speech) is the service specifically designed to convert written text into spoken words, making it the perfect fit for reading recipe instructions aloud.

Reference:

https://azure.microsoft.com/en-us/services/cognitive-services/text-to-speech/#features

12) Correct answer:

Answer Area

Statements	Yes	No
You can use the Speech service to transcribe a call to text.	◉	○
You can use the Text Analytics service to extract key entities from a call transcript.	◉	○
You can use the Speech service to translate the audio of a call to a different language.	◉	○

Transcribe a call to text-Speech Service: Speech to Text Service

Extract call Transcription to find key entity - Text Analytic: Entity Recognition

Translate a call to different language: Speech Service: Speech Translations.

Here are the answers to each statement:

Yes. The Speech service offers speech-to-text conversion, which can transcribe audio from a call into text format.

Yes. Text Analytics can analyze text data, including call transcripts. Its functionality includes key phrase extraction and entity recognition, which can be used to identify important details and entities mentioned in the call.

Yes. The Speech service also offers real-time speech translation capabilities. You can translate the audio of a call directly into a different language.

References:

https://learn.microsoft.com/en-us/azure/ai-services/speech-service/overview

https://docs.microsoft.com/en-gb/azure/cognitive-services/text-analytics/overview

https://azure.microsoft.com/en-gb/services/cognitive-services/speech-services/

13) The best AI workload to detect customer sentiment in chat messages is:

D. Natural Language Processing (NLP)

Here's why the other options are incorrect:

Anomaly detection: This is used for identifying unusual patterns in data. While unusual language patterns might be indicative of an upset customer, it's not the most specific approach for understanding the sentiment behind the text.

Semantic segmentation: This is a computer vision technique for classifying pixels in an image. It wouldn't be applicable to analyzing text data from a chatbot conversation.

Regression: This is used for predicting a continuous value based on input features. While it might be used in sentiment analysis systems that assign a numerical score, NLP is the broader field that encompasses techniques for understanding and analyzing the emotional tone of text.

NLP specifically deals with tasks like sentiment analysis, which involves analyzing text data to determine the emotional tone or opinion expressed. This perfectly aligns with the need to detect when a customer is upset based on their chat messages.

Natural language processing (NLP) is used for tasks such as sentiment analysis, topic detection, language detection, key phrase extraction, and document categorization.

Sentiment Analysis is the process of determining whether a

piece of writing is positive, negative or neutral.

Reference:

https://docs.microsoft.com/en-us/azure/architecture/data-guide/technology-choices/natural-language-processing

14) The two key services required for this solution are:

A. QnA Maker

B. Azure Bot Service

Here's why these options are the best fit:

QnA Maker: This service is specifically designed for creating and managing a knowledge base of question-answer pairs. It allows users to ask questions in natural language and retrieves the most relevant answer from the knowledge base.

Azure Bot Service: This service provides a framework for building intelligent bots that can interact with users through various channels (web chat, messaging apps, etc.). It allows you to integrate QnA Maker with your bot so users can interact with the knowledge base conversationally.

Let's look at why the other options are not ideal for this scenario:

C. Form Recognizer: This service is used to extract information from forms and documents. While it might be helpful for processing specific data formats within the knowledge base, it's not directly related to facilitating natural language queries.

D. Anomaly Detector: This service identifies unusual patterns in data. It wouldn't be directly applicable to building a bot that interacts with a knowledge base through natural language.

References:

https://docs.microsoft.com/en-us/azure/bot-service/bot-service-overview-introduction?view=azure-bot-service-4.0

https://docs.microsoft.com/en-us/azure/cognitive-services/luis/choose-natural-language-processing-service

15) Here are three ways to create question and answer text using QnA Maker:

A. Generate the questions and answers from an existing webpage: This is a valid approach. QnA Maker can extract questions and answers from existing webpages. You can point it to the relevant webpage, and it will try to identify potential question-answer pairs based on the content structure.

C. Manually enter the questions and answers: This is also a viable option. QnA Maker provides a user interface where you can directly enter the question-and-answer pairs for your knowledge base. This allows for full control over the content and is suitable for smaller datasets or when specific phrasing is important.

E. Import chit-chat content from a predefined data source: QnA Maker offers pre-built content sets for common chit-chat scenarios like greetings, small talk, and basic troubleshooting. This can be a good starting point for adding a layer of personality and friendliness to your chatbot.

Here's why the other options are not suitable for creating question and answer text:

B. Use automated machine learning to train a model based on a file that contains the questions: While QnA Maker does leverage machine learning for ranking and improving responses, it doesn't require a separate training step. You directly provide the question-answer pairs, and the service uses its algorithms to understand the content and relationships.

D. Connect the bot to the Cortana channel and ask questions by using Cortana: This describes interacting with a built chatbot, not creating the content for it. While connecting your bot to the Cortana channel might be part of the deployment process, it doesn't contribute to creating the QnA knowledge base itself.

Automatic extraction

Extract question-answer pairs from semi-structured content, including FAQ pages, support websites, excel files, SharePoint documents, product manuals and policies.

Reference:

https://docs.microsoft.com/en-us/azure/cognitive-services/qnamaker/concepts/content-types

16) The best service for creating a conversational support system based on an FAQ is:

A. QnA Maker

Here's why the other options are not ideal:

B. Text Analytics: This service is for analyzing text data and wouldn't directly translate to building a conversational system. While it might be used for preliminary tasks like extracting questions and answers from the PDF, it wouldn't handle the conversational interaction aspect.

C. Computer Vision: This service deals with analyzing visual information like images and wouldn't be applicable to processing text data from a PDF FAQ.

D. Language Understanding (LUIS): LUIS is designed to understand the intent behind natural language used in applications. While it might be useful in more complex chatbots that require understanding user goals, QnA Maker is specifically built for creating knowledge bases of question-answer pairs, making it a better fit for a conversational FAQ system.

QnA Maker is a cloud-based API service that lets you create a conversational question-and-answer layer over your existing data. Use it to build a knowledge base by extracting questions and answers from your semi-structured content, including FAQs, manuals, and documents.

Reference:

https://azure.microsoft.com/en-us/services/cognitive-services/qna-maker/

17) Here are the two AI services you should use to achieve the goal:

B. QnA Maker

C. Azure Bot Service

Let's see why these options are the best fit:

QnA Maker: This service is crucial for building the knowledge base that stores the predefined answers to the simple questions. You can create a knowledge base in QnA Maker by providing question-answer pairs, potentially extracted from existing FAQs or manually entered.

Azure Bot Service: This service allows you to build the chatbot itself. You can integrate the QnA Maker knowledge base with the bot, enabling it to retrieve and deliver the appropriate answers to user queries phrased in natural language.

Here's why the other options are not ideal:

A. Text Analytics: While Text Analytics can be used for analyzing text data, it wouldn't directly create a chatbot or knowledge base. It might be helpful for pre-processing tasks like cleaning the FAQ data before feeding it into QnA Maker.

D. Translator Text: This service translates text from one language to another. While the chatbot might need translation capabilities in some scenarios, the primary focus here is understanding predefined questions and delivering predefined answers, making QnA Maker and Azure Bot Service the more relevant choices.

Bots are a popular way to provide support through multiple communication channels. You can use the QnA Maker service and Azure Bot Service to create a bot that answers user questions.

Reference:

https://docs.microsoft.com/en-us/learn/modules/build-faq-chatbot-qna-maker-azure-bot-service/

18) Correct answer: A. Copilots

Copilots are frequently incorporated into applications to offer users a means of seeking assistance with routine tasks from a generative AI model. Because they are built on a standardized architecture, developers can create customized copilots for different business-specific applications and services.

Reference:

What are copilots?

The availability of LLMs has led to the emergence of a new category of computing known as copilots. Copilots are often integrated into other applications and provide a way for users to get help with common tasks from a generative AI model. Copilots are based on a common architecture, so developers can build custom copilots for various business-specific applications and services.

You may see copilots appear within the products that you already use, for example, as a chat screen feature that opens up next to your file. These copilots use the content that is created or searched for in the product as specific information for its results.

It's helpful to think of how the creation of a large language model is related to the process of creating a copilot application:

A large amount of data is used to train a large language model.

Services such as Azure OpenAI Service make pretrained models available. Developers can use these pretrained models as they are, or fine-tune them with custom data.

Deploying a model makes it available for use in applications.

Developers can build copilots that submit prompts to models and generate content for use in applications.

Business users can use copilots to boost their productivity and creativity with AI-generated content.

Copilots have the potential to revolutionize the way we work by helping with first drafts, information synthesis, strategic planning, and much more.

https://learn.microsoft.com/en-us/training/modules/fundamentals-generative-ai/5-copilots

19) This is an example of a:

B. chatbot

Here's why the other options are incorrect:

A. sentiment analysis solution - Sentiment analysis is a type of NLP that analyzes text to determine the emotional tone. While chatbots may use sentiment analysis to understand user intent, the core function in the image is answering questions about using REST APIs, not sentiment analysis.

C. machine learning model - Machine learning models are algorithms trained on data to make predictions or classifications. While chatbots may use machine learning models under the hood, the image itself doesn't directly show the training or prediction aspects of a machine learning model. It focuses on the conversational interaction between the user and the chatbot.

D. computer vision application - Computer vision deals with analyzing visual information from images or videos. There is no image or video processing involved in the chat interaction shown in the image.

20) The most suitable service for this scenario is:

B. QnA Maker

Here's why the other options are not ideal for this task:

A. Custom Vision: This service is designed for building custom image recognition models. While it might be useful in some customer support scenarios (e.g., identifying product images from user queries), the primary focus here is text-based interaction and guiding users to resources or answers, making QnA Maker a better fit. Azure Custom Vision is a cognitive service that lets you build, deploy, and improve your own image classifiers. An image classifier is an AI service that applies labels (which represent classes) to images, according to their visual characteristics. Unlike the Computer Vision service, Custom Vision allows you to specify the labels to apply.

C. Translator Text: This service translates text from one language to another. While translation might be necessary in some cases, the core functionality here is understanding user queries and directing them to the best resource, not translation itself.

D. Face: This service detects human faces in images. Similar to Custom Vision, it wouldn't directly address the need for a text-based conversational support system that guides users to resources or answers. Azure Cognitive Services Face Detection API: At a minimum, each detected face corresponds to a face Rectangle field in the response. This set of pixel coordinates for the left, top, width, and height mark the located face. Using these coordinates, you can get the location of the face and its size. In the API response, faces are listed in size order from largest to smallest.

QnA Maker allows you to create a knowledge base of question-answer pairs. You can integrate this knowledge base with a web application, enabling users to interact with the system and receive answers to their questions or be directed to the most relevant resources.

QnA Maker is a cloud-based API service that lets you create a conversational question-and-answer layer over your existing data. Use it to build a knowledge base by extracting questions and answers from your semi-structured content, including FAQs, manuals, and documents. Answer users questions with the best answers from the QnAs in your knowledge base automatically. Your knowledge base gets smarter, too, as it continually learns from user behavior.

Reference:

https://azure.microsoft.com/en-us/services/cognitive-services/qna-maker/

21) The best AI service to create a bot from a Frequently Asked Questions (FAQ) document is:

A. QnA Maker

Here's why the other options are not ideal for this task:

B. Language Understanding (LUIS): LUIS is designed to understand the intent behind natural language used in applications. While it might be useful for more complex chatbots that require understanding user goals beyond simple FAQs, QnA Maker is specifically built for creating knowledge bases of question-answer pairs, making it a better fit for this scenario.

C. Text Analytics: Text Analytics can analyze text data and might be helpful for pre-processing the FAQ document (e.g., cleaning or structuring the data) before feeding it into QnA Maker. However, it wouldn't directly create a bot itself.

D. Speech: Speech recognition can convert spoken words to text.

While a chatbot might use speech recognition to understand user queries phrased as spoken language, QnA Maker focuses on building the knowledge base that stores the answers to the FAQs, regardless of whether the questions are presented in text or speech.

22) Correct Answer:

Answer Area

The interactive answering of questions entered by a user as part of an application is an example of

anomaly detection.
computer vision.
conversational AI.
forecasting.

With Microsoft Conversational AI tools developers can build, connect, deploy, and manage intelligent bots that naturally interact with their users on a website, app, Cortana, Microsoft Teams, Skype, Facebook Messenger, Slack, and more.

conversational AI is the correct overarching concept.

QnA Maker is a specific tool that falls under the umbrella of conversational AI. Conversational AI refers to the broader field of technologies that enable machines to simulate human conversation through speech or text. QnA Maker helps you build a chatbot, which is one application of conversational AI.

So, while both conversational AI and QnA Maker are relevant terms, conversational AI provides a more general understanding of the technology involved, while QnA Maker refers to a specific service for building a particular type of conversational

AI system (a chatbot focused on answering questions from a knowledge base).

Reference:
https://azure.microsoft.com/en-in/blog/microsoft-conversational-ai-tools-enable-developers-to-build-connect-and-manage-intelligent-bots

23) The scenario that is an example of a webchat bot is:

D. From a website interface, answer common questions about scheduled events and ticket purchases for a music festival.

Here's why the other options are not examples of webchat bots:

A. Determine whether reviews entered on a website for a concert are positive or negative, and then add a thumbs up or thumbs down emoji to the reviews. This describes sentiment analysis, a type of NLP task, but it doesn't involve interacting with users in a chat-like interface.

B. Translate into English questions entered by customers at a kiosk so that the appropriate person can call the customers back. This scenario involves machine translation, but it doesn't directly interact with users in a conversational manner.

C. Accept questions through email, and then route the email messages to the correct person based on the content of the message. This describes an email routing system based on content analysis, not a conversational interaction through a chat window.

A webchat bot is a computer program that simulates conversation with users through a website interface. It typically uses natural language processing to understand user queries and provide relevant responses.

In scenario D, the bot directly interacts with users on the website interface, answering their questions about the music festival in a conversational way. This aligns perfectly with the definition of a webchat bot.

24) Correct Answer:

Answer Area

Statements	Yes	No
You can use QnA Maker to query an Azure SQL database.	○	●
You should use QnA Maker when you want a knowledge base to provide the same answer to different users who submit similar questions.	●	○
The QnA Maker service can determine the intent of a user utterance.	○	●

Here are the answers to each statement:

1. No. QnA Maker is specifically designed for working with knowledge bases of question-answer pairs. It cannot directly query an Azure SQL database. You would need a separate service or tool to connect to and query the database.

2. Yes. QnA Maker excels at providing consistent responses to similar user queries. When you create your knowledge base, you can add multiple question variations that map to the same answer. This ensures users get the same information regardless of how they phrase their question.

3. No. QnA Maker focuses on exact matching or keyword-based retrieval within the knowledge base. It doesn't have the capability to understand the deeper intent behind a user's question, which is a more advanced NLP task.

Reference:

https://docs.microsoft.com/en-gb/azure/cognitive-services/qnamaker/concepts/data-sources-and-content

https://docs.microsoft.com/en-us/azure/cognitive-services/luis/choose-natural-language-processing-service

25) Correct Answer:

Answer Area

Statements	Yes	No
You can communicate with a bot by using email.	○	
You can communicate with a bot by using Microsoft Teams.	○	
You can communicate with a bot by using a webchat interface.	○	

1. Yes: You can communicate with a bot using email if the bot is configured to accept and respond to emails.

2. Yes: You can communicate with a bot using Microsoft Teams if the bot is integrated into Teams as a chatbot.

3. Yes: You can communicate with a bot using a webchat interface if the bot is embedded on a website or web application.

Reference:
https://docs.microsoft.com/en-us/azure/bot-service/bot-service-manage-channels?view=azure-bot-service-4.0

26) Correct Answer:

Answer Area

Statements	Yes	No
A restaurant can use a chatbot to empower customers to make reservations by using a website or an app.	○	○
A restaurant can use a chatbot to answer inquiries about business hours from a webpage.	○	○
A restaurant can use a chatbot to automate responses to customer reviews on an external website.	○	○

1. Yes: A restaurant can use a chatbot on their website or app to allow customers to make reservations easily.

2. Yes: A chatbot can be used on a webpage to answer common questions about the restaurant's business hours.

3. Yes: A chatbot can be used to automatically respond to customer reviews on external websites, providing timely feedback and engagement.

Reference: https://docs.microsoft.com/en-us/azure/bot-service/bot-service-overview-introduction?view=azure-bot-service-4.0

27) Here are the two scenarios that exemplify conversational AI workloads:

B. a chatbot that provides users with the ability to find answers on a website by themselves

C. telephone voice menus to reduce the load on human resources

Conversational AI workloads involve interactions between humans and machines using natural language.

B. A chatbot that assists users in finding answers falls under this category. It leverages natural language processing to understand user queries and guide them towards relevant information on the website. A bot is an automated software program designed to perform a particular task. Think of it as a robot without a body.

C. Telephone voice menus that use speech recognition and pre-recorded prompts also qualify as conversational AI. Users interact with the system through spoken language to navigate options and potentially reach the information they need without requiring a human representative. Automated customer interaction is essential to a business of any size. In fact, 61% of consumers prefer to communicate via speech, and most of them prefer self-service. Because customer satisfaction is a priority for all businesses, self-service is a critical facet of any customer-facing communications strategy.

Let's look at why the other options are not conversational AI:

A. A telephone answering service with a pre-recorded message: This is a one-way communication method. While it might be part of a larger system that includes human interaction, the pre-recorded message itself doesn't involve natural language processing or user interaction.

D. A service that creates FAQs by crawling public websites: This describes a content creation process, not an interactive system that uses natural language for communication. It might be a useful tool for populating a chatbot's knowledge base, but it's not a conversational AI workload itself.

Early bots were comparatively simple, handling repetitive and voluminous tasks with relatively straightforward algorithmic logic. An example would be web crawlers used by search engines to automatically explore and catalog web content.

References:

https://docs.microsoft.com/en-us/azure/architecture/data-guide/big-data/ai-overview

https://docs.microsoft.com/en-us/azure/architecture/solution-ideas/articles/interactive-voice-response-bot

28) Correct Answer:

Answer Area		
Statements	Yes	No
Azure Bot Service and Azure Congnitive Services can be integrated.	O	o
Azure Bot Service engages with customers in a conversational manner.	O	o
Azure Bot Service can import frequently asked questions (FAQ) to question and answer sets.	o	O

Box 1: Yes

Azure bot service can be integrated with the powerful AI capabilities with Azure Cognitive Services.

Box 2: Yes

Azure bot service engages with customers in a conversational manner.

Box 3: No

The QnA Maker service creates knowledge base, not question and answers sets.

While Azure Bot Service can import and use frequently asked questions (FAQs) to improve its responses, it does not directly import them into question-and-answer sets. Developers need to structure the FAQ content in a way that the bot can understand and use effectively.

Note: You can use the QnA Maker service and a knowledge

base to add question-and-answer support to your bot. When you create your knowledge base, you seed it with questions and answers.

YES, YES and NO respectively since the BOT has to be pointed to the QnA maker.

References:

You can easily create a user support bot solution on Microsoft Azure using a combination of two core services:

- Language service. The Language service includes a custom question answering feature that enables you to create a knowledge base of question-and-answer pairs that can be queried using natural language input.

- Azure Bot service. This service provides a framework for developing, publishing, and managing bots on Azure.

https://docs.microsoft.com/en-us/azure/bot-service/bot-builder-tutorial-add-qna

https://learn.microsoft.com/en-us/training/modules/build-faq-chatbot-qna-maker-azure-bot-service/2-get-started-knowledge-base

29) The best option to improve the relevance of responses in your webchat bot using user feedback is:

D. Active learning

Here's why the other options are not as suitable for this scenario:

A. key phrase extraction can be helpful for understanding the main topics users are asking about, but it doesn't directly address improving the relevance of specific responses based on user feedback.

B. sentiment analysis can tell you if users are happy or frustrated with the bot's responses, but it doesn't necessarily pinpoint which answers need improvement.

C. Business logic defines the rules and processes the bot follows, but it wouldn't directly use user feedback to improve the QnA Maker knowledge base.

Active learning is a machine learning technique where the model actively seeks out new data points to improve its performance. In the context of your chatbot, active learning can be used to identify areas where the bot's responses are not meeting user expectations.

Here's how it might work:

When a user expresses dissatisfaction with a response, the bot could prompt them for additional information about what they were looking for. This feedback can be used to:

Identify the specific QnA Maker answer pair that needs improvement.

Train the QnA Maker knowledge base to better understand similar questions in the future.

By iteratively using active learning with user feedback, the QnA Maker knowledge base can be continuously refined, leading to more relevant and helpful responses for users.

Reference:

https://docs.microsoft.com/en-us/azure/cognitive-services/qnamaker/how-to/improve-knowledge-base

30) The best service for developing a conversational AI solution that communicates across multiple channels is:

B. Azure Bot Service

Here's why the other options are not ideal for this scenario:

A. Text Analytics: This service is primarily used for analyzing text data, not building chatbots. While it might be helpful for pre-processing text from emails or other sources, it wouldn't handle the core conversation management aspect.

C. Translator: This service translates text from one language to another. While translation might be necessary for a multilingual chatbot, it's not the primary functionality here. You need a framework for building the bot itself that can interact with users across channels.

D. Form Recognizer: This service extracts information from forms and documents. While it might be useful for specific scenarios involving structured data, it's not designed for building conversational AI systems.

Azure Bot Service provides a comprehensive platform for developing intelligent bots. It allows you to:

Design the conversation flow of your bot.

Integrate with various channels like email, Microsoft Teams, and webchat.

Connect the bot to knowledge bases like QnA Maker for answering user questions.

This makes Azure Bot Service the ideal choice for building a multi-channel conversational AI solution.

Reference:

https://docs.microsoft.com/en-us/azure/bot-service/bot-service-overview-introduction?view=azure-bot-service-4.0

31) Correct Answers are:

Here's the breakdown of each statement:

1. Yes

A bot that responds to queries by internal users is an example of a conversational AI workload.

Conversational AI involves interactions between humans and machines using natural language. Even though the users are internal, the bot is still using natural language processing to understand their queries and provide responses.

2. No

An application that displays images relating to an entered search term is an example of image search, not a conversational AI workload.

Conversational AI requires interaction through natural language. While the user might enter a search term, the application isn't using natural language processing to understand the intent or respond conversationally.

3. No

A web form used to submit a request to reset a password is not a conversational AI workload.

Conversational AI involves back-and-forth communication. A web form is a static interface where users fill in information, not a conversational interaction.

32) Correct answer: C. safety system

The safety system layer consists of platform-level settings and features that help reduce harm. For instance, the Azure OpenAI service offers content filters that use specific criteria to hide prompts and responses based on the classification of content into four severity levels (safe, low, medium, and high) across four categories of potential harm (hate, sexual, violence, and self-harm).

Reference:

https://learn.microsoft.com/en-us/training/modules/responsible-generative-ai/5-mitigate-harms

33) Correct Answers: D

The principle for Responsible AI that you complied with by providing information about the solution's possibilities and limitations is:

D. Transparency

Here's why transparency is the most fitting answer:

Responsible AI emphasizes the importance of openness and clear communication about AI systems.

By explaining your solution's capabilities and limitations, you are setting expectations for users and stakeholders.

This transparency allows users to understand what the AI solution can and cannot do, fostering trust and responsible use.

The other options you might consider are not as directly related to transparency in this scenario:

Fairness focuses on ensuring AI solutions avoid discrimination or bias.

Reliability and safety address the need for AI systems to function predictably and avoid causing harm.

Privacy and security deal with protecting user data and ensuring its responsible use.

Inclusiveness emphasizes designing AI systems that consider diverse user needs and perspectives.

Accountability refers to taking responsibility for the development, deployment, and impacts of AI systems.

While these principles are all important in Responsible AI, explaining the solution's possibilities and limitations directly addresses the concept of transparency.

Microsoft recognizes six principles of responsible AI:

Fairness, Reliability and safety, Privacy and security Transparency, Inclusiveness Accountability.

The principle of Transparency helps people to understand how to use AI solutions, their behavior, possibilities, and limitations.

All other options are incorrect:

For more information about guiding principles for responsible AI, please visit the below URLs"

https//wwwmicrosoftcom/en-us/ai/responsible-ai?activetab=pivotl:primaryra

https//docsmicrosoftcom/en-us/Learn/modules/responsibLe-ai-principles/4-guiding-principles

34) Correct Answers: B

No, an unsupervised machine learning approach wouldn't be the most suitable method for predicting the number of blue cars to order.

Here's why:

Unsupervised learning: This approach is ideal for identifying patterns and hidden structures in unlabeled data. It doesn't involve predicting a specific target variable.

Goal: You want to predict the number of blue cars to order (a specific target variable).

Here's a better approach:

Supervised learning: This method involves training a model on historical data where you have both the features (e.g., car color, model, sales history) and the target variable (e.g., number of cars sold). The model learns the relationship between features and the target variable and can then be used to predict the target variable for new, unseen data.

In this scenario, you could use supervised learning to create a model that predicts car sales based on factors like color, model, and past sales data. This model could then be used to estimate the number of blue cars to order for the next quarter.

Your task is to provide a numeric prediction. You can achieve this by creating a regression model based on the historical sales data of the blue cars from previous quarters A Regression and Classification modeling types are two parts of Supervised machine learning. Only Clustering belongs to Unsupervised machine Learning. If you choose the Unsupervised machine

Learning approach, you will not achieve your goal.

For more information about Supervised and Unsupervised ML. please visit the below URI_:

https//azure.microsoft.com/en-us/overview/what-is-machine-learning-platform/#benefits

35) Correct Answers: D

In this scenario, the most important pre-processing step to predict the success of the new car model is:

D. Feature selection

Here's why:

Feature selection involves identifying the most relevant data points (features) from your dataset that will influence the model's ability to predict success.

In this case, you have compiled data about previous successful models, including characteristics like engine improvements, seat comfort, sunroof presence, and likely sales numbers.

By selecting the most relevant features that have a strong correlation with sales success, you can create a more accurate model for predicting the new model's performance.

Let's explore why the other options are not the primary focus here:

A. Data selection: While data selection is a broader step in pre-processing, feature selection specifically focuses on choosing the most relevant features within the selected data.

B. Training set selection: This would be a later step where

you divide your data into training and testing sets for model development and evaluation.

C. Data for model evaluation selection: Similar to training set selection, this comes after feature selection when you prepare data to assess the model's performance.

E. Data classification: This might be necessary if you're categorizing success levels (e.g., high, medium, low sales), but feature selection remains the crucial step for identifying the impactful characteristics that influence that classification.

Therefore, focusing on feature selection in the pre-processing stage will help you build a more effective model for predicting the success of the new car model based on relevant historical data.

During pre-processing. you need to work with data to select features that influence the Label prediction. In this problem, features are the engine characteristics (power or volume). seat comforts, etc. They could help the ML model to predict the success of the new car model Maybe the sunroof is not essential for predicting the Label, and we need to discard this feature from the final set of features that we will use for model training.

In short, Feature selection helps us to narrow down the features that are important for our Label prediction and discard all features that don't play or play a minimal role in a Label prediction. As a result, our trained model and prediction will be more efficient.

ALL other options are incorrect because they are parts of the different data processing events that are irrelevant to the pre-processing (Training set selection or Data for model evaluation selection) or too generic (Data selection or Data Classification).

For more information about Feature selection, please visit the below URL https//docsmicrosoftcom/en-us/azure/machine-learning/team-data-science-process/select-features

36) Correct Answers: C

The size of the confusion matrix for a classification model with four possible classes will be:

C. 4x4

Here's why:

A confusion matrix is a table that shows the performance of a classification model.

It has rows representing the actual classes (ground truth) and columns representing the predicted classes by the model.

Since you have four possible classes, the rows and columns will each have four categories, resulting in a 4x4 matrix.

Each cell of the matrix represents the number of instances where a specific class was:

Predicted correctly (diagonal)

Predicted incorrectly (off-diagonal)

For example, one cell might show how many instances from class A were actually classified as class B by the model.

The size of the confusion matrix grows with the number of classes. So, for a model with two classes, you'd have a 2x2 matrix, and for six classes, it would be a 6x6 matrix.

The confusion matrix provides a tabulated view of predicted and actual values for each class. If we are predicting the classification for four classes, our confusion matrix will have

4x4 size.

ALL other options are incorrect.

For more information about the Confusion matrix, please visit the below URL:

https//docsmicrosoftcom/en-us/azure/machine-learning/how-to-understand-automated-ml#confusion-matrix

37) Correct Answers: D

The generic name for the process that includes selecting labels, features, scaling, and normalizing them during data preparation for model training is:

D. Featurization

Here's a breakdown of why featurization is the most suitable term:

Featurization: This term encompasses the entire process of transforming raw data into features that a machine learning model can understand and use for training. It involves:

Label selection: Choosing the target variable you want the model to predict (e.g., customer churn, image classification category).

Feature selection: Identifying the most relevant data points from the raw data that will influence the model's ability to learn and predict.

Scaling and normalization: Transforming the features to a common scale or distribution to ensure all features contribute equally during model training.

The other options focus on specific aspects of featurization:

A. Feature selection: This is a step within featurization, not the overarching process. Feature selections is one of the elements of featurization.

B. Data normalization: This is a specific technique used during featurization for scaling features. Data normalization is also one of the elements of featurization.

C. Model training: This is a separate stage that comes after data preparation (featurization). Model Training is the next predictive modeling step after featurization.

E. Missing data handling: This is an important aspect of data cleaning, which is often a preliminary step before featurization. Missing data handling is one of the elements of featurization.

Therefore, featurization captures the comprehensive process of preparing data for machine learning models by transforming raw data into features suitable for model training.

Data pre-processing that involves various techniques, like scaling, normalization or feature engineering, etc. calls featurization.

For more information about Featurization, please visit the below URLs:

https//docsmicrosoftcom/en-us/azure/machine-learning/concept-automated-ml#feature-engineering

https//docsmicrosoftcom/en-us/azure/machine-learning/how-to-configure-auto-features#featurization

38) Correct answer: C. Generative AI

Generative AI models, like DALL-E, can generate images based on textual prompts, showcasing their ability to create visual content from natural language input. Other AI capabilities serve diverse purposes in varying contexts, each tailored to achieve specific objectives.

Reference:

What is generative AI?

Artificial Intelligence (AI) imitates human behavior by using machine learning to interact with the environment and execute tasks without explicit directions on what to output.

Generative AI describes a category of capabilities within AI that create original content. People typically interact with generative AI that has been built into chat applications. One popular example of such an application is ChatGPT, a chatbot created by OpenAI, an AI research company that partners closely with Microsoft.

Generative AI applications take in natural language input, and return appropriate responses in a variety of formats such as natural language, images, or code.

https://learn.microsoft.com/en-us/training/modules/fundamentals-generative-ai/2-what-is-generative-ai

39) Correct Answers: C. System messages.

System messages are employed to establish the context for the model, outlining expectations and guiding its responses to prompts. While other techniques are utilized in generative AI models, they serve different purposes in varying use cases.

Reference:

Prompt engineering techniques include defining a system message. The message sets the context for the model by describing expectations and constraints, for example, "You're a helpful assistant that responds in a cheerful, friendly manner". These system messages determine constraints and styles for the model's responses.

https://learn.microsoft.com/en-us/training/modules/fundamentals-generative-ai/6-writing-prompts

40) Correct Answers: A, C, D, and F.

A. Project ID: Identifies the specific Custom Vision project containing your model.

C. Model name: Specifies the name of the Custom Vision model you created.

D. Prediction key: A key that allows your application to authenticate and access the Custom Vision service for predictions.

E. Prediction Endpoint: The URL endpoint where your application can send requests to get predictions from your Custom Vision model.

If you create a Cognitive Service to train and publish the Custom Vision model, you can provide a Cognitive Service endpoint and Cognitive Service key to the developers for access to the model. But if you use the Custom Vision portal or create a Custom Vision resource within Cognitive Service, you will have two separate resources for training and publishing a model in this case, you need to provide the four pieces of information to the developers:

Project ID. Model name, Prediction Key, and Prediction Endpoint

Option B is incorrect since Security Key is just a generic key that isn't applicable in this case.

Option E is incorrect since we need to provide the pair: Cognitive Service endpoint and Cognitive Service key Only one of them, a Cognitive Service key, will not work.

For more information about Custom Vision, please visit the below URLs:

https//docsmicrosoftcom/en-us/azure/cognitive-services/custom-vision-service/home

41) Correct answers are:

A. a webpage.

C. an existing FAQ document.

E. manually entered data.

You can create a knowledge base by extracting question-and-answer pairs from a webpage or an existing document, such as a text file. Alternatively, you can manually input the question-and-answer pairs. Importing a knowledge base directly from an image or an audio file is not possible.

Reference:

https://learn.microsoft.com/en-us/training/modules/build-faq-chatbot-qna-maker-azure-bot-service/

42) Correct answer: A. Identify potential harms.

The initial stage for crafting a responsible generative AI solution using the NIST AI RMF involves identifying potential harms.

Here's the breakdown of why this is the first step:

NIST AI RMF emphasizes trustworthiness: The framework focuses on building trust in AI systems by managing risks throughout the lifecycle.

Generative AI poses unique risks: These systems can create realistic but potentially harmful content, so identifying these risks upfront is crucial.

Proactive risk management: By identifying potential harms early on, organizations can take steps to mitigate them before deployment.

Therefore, identifying potential harms lays the foundation for developing a responsible generative AI solution using the NIST AI RMF.

The other answer choices follow later stages in the risk management process:

Measure the presence of potential harms: This might occur after identifying potential harms to assess their likelihood and severity.

Mitigate potential harms: This involves taking steps to reduce the identified risks.

Operate the solution: This is the final stage where the AI system is deployed and monitored.

Reference:

The potential harms that are relevant to your generative AI

solution depend on multiple factors, including the specific services and models used to generate output as well as any fine-tuning or grounding data used to customize the outputs. Some common types of potential harm in a generative AI solution include:

Generating content that is offensive, pejorative, or discriminatory.

Generating content that contains factual inaccuracies.

Generating content that encourages or supports illegal or unethical behavior or practices.

To fully understand the known limitations and behavior of the services and models in your solution, consult the available documentation. For example, the Azure OpenAI Service includes a transparency note; which you can use to understand specific considerations related to the service and the models it includes. Additionally, individual model developers may provide documentation such as the OpenAI system card for the GPT-4 model.

https://learn.microsoft.com/en-us/training/modules/responsible-generative-ai/2-plan-responsible-ai

43) Correct answers are:

A. Create natural language.

E. Understand natural language.

Azure OpenAI natural language models are capable of processing natural language input and producing corresponding responses. GPT models excel at comprehending and generating natural language.

Reference:

Understand OpenAI's natural language capabilities:

Azure OpenAI's natural language models are able to take in natural language and generate responses.

Natural language learning models are trained on words or chunks of characters known as tokens. For example, the word "hamburger" gets broken up into the tokens ham, bur, and ger, while a short and common word like "pear" is a single token. These tokens are mapped into vectors for a machine learning model to use for training. When a trained natural language model takes in a user's input, it also breaks down the input into tokens.

Understanding GPT models for natural language generation:

Generative pre-trained transformer (GPT) models are excellent at both understanding and creating natural language. If you've seen recent news around AI answering questions or writing a paragraph based on a prompt, it likely could have been generated by a GPT model such as GPT-35-Turbo or GPT-4.

https://learn.microsoft.com/en-us/training/modules/explore-azure-openai/5-understand-openai-natural-language

44) Correct answers are:

B. creating variations of an image.

C. editing an image.

E. new image creation.

Out of the given options, three functionalities exemplify image generation features in a generative AI model:

B. Creating variations of an image: Generative AI models excel at manipulating existing data. They can be used to create different versions of an image, such as changing the style (e.g., making a portrait look like a painting), altering specific elements (e.g., adding a hat to a person), or generating similar scenes with variations.

C. Editing an image: While some editing tasks might involve specific software, generative AI models can be used for content-aware editing. This means they can understand the content of an image and make edits that appear natural, such as removing objects seamlessly or adding realistic elements.

E. New image creation: This is the core functionality of image generation in generative AI models. Based on text descriptions, prompts, or even reference images, the model can create entirely new images that are original and relevant to the input.

Here's why the other options are not functionalities of image generation:

A. Animation of static images: While some generative AI models might be used in conjunction with animation techniques, creating animations from static images is a separate process.

D. Extracting RGB values from an image: This is a basic image processing task that doesn't involve creating new visual content.

Generative AI models for image generation can use a prompt, a base image, or both to produce novel outputs. These models are capable of generating realistic and artistic images, altering an image's layout or style, and creating different versions of a given image.

Reference:

Original images can be generated by providing a text prompt of what you would like the image to be of. The more detailed the prompt, the more likely the model will provide a desired result.

With DALL-E, you can even request an image in a particular style, such as "a dog in the style of Vincent van Gogh". Styles can be used for edits and variations as well.

https://learn.microsoft.com/en-us/training/modules/explore-azure-openai/7-understand-openai-image-generation

45) Correct answer: A. image description.

DALL-E does not include the capability for image description, meaning this use case cannot be implemented using DALL-E. However, the other three capabilities are available in DALL-E through Azure OpenAI.

Reference:

https://learn.microsoft.com/en-us/training/modules/explore-azure-openai/7-understand-openai-image-generation

46) Correct answer: A. DALL-E

DALL-E is capable of generating images based on natural language input. GPT-4 and GPT-3.5 excel at understanding and generating natural language and code, but they do not process images. Embeddings convert text into numerical vectors to enable text similarity comparisons. Whisper is designed to transcribe and translate speech into text.

Here's why DALL-E is the best choice:

DALL-E focuses on image generation: This model is known for its ability to create high-quality and realistic images based on text descriptions. It can interpret complex concepts and translate them into visual forms.

Natural language understanding: DALL-E is trained on a massive dataset of text and images, allowing it to understand the nuances of human language and generate visuals that align with the intended meaning.

Here's why the other options are not as relevant:

B. Embeddings: Embeddings are a technique used in natural language processing (NLP) to represent words or phrases as numerical vectors. While they can be helpful for AI models that handle text data, embeddings themselves don't generate images.

C. GPT-3.5 and D. GPT-4: These are large language models primarily focused on generating text. While they might be able to describe images in words, they are not specifically designed to create visual content.

E. Whisper: Whisper is an automatic speech recognition model, not an image generation model. It excels at transcribing audio into text.

References:

https://learn.microsoft.com/en-us/training/modules/explore-azure-openai/7-understand-openai-image-generation

https://chatgpt.com/c/38d7da22-cba7-43dc-af63-702d755f30a9

47) Correct answer: D. removing stop words

The initial step in the statistical analysis of terms in a text in the context of NLP is to eliminate stop words. Once stop words are removed, the next step involves counting the occurrences of each word. While creating a vectorized model is not part of statistical analysis, it is employed to capture the semantic relationships between words. Similarly, encoding words as numeric features is not part of statistical analysis but is commonly used in sentiment analysis.

Reference:

https://learn.microsoft.com/en-us/training/modules/analyze-text-with-text-analytics-service/1-introduction

48) Correct answer: C. NaN

The confidence score provided by the Azure AI Language Detection service in NLP for an unidentified language is C. NaN.

Here's why:

NaN stands for "Not a Number": This is a special value used in computing to indicate that a value is unavailable or undefined.

Unidentified language: When the Language Detection service cannot definitively identify a language, it cannot assign a specific confidence score.

Transparency in results: By returning NaN, the service acknowledges the limitation and avoids providing a misleading confidence value.

This approach ensures clarity and allows developers to handle unidentified languages appropriately in their applications.

NaN, which stands for not a number, represents an unknown

confidence score in this context. The term "unknown" is used to describe the condition associated with the NaN confidence score. Confidence scores range from 0 to 1, with 0 indicating the lowest confidence and 1 indicating the highest confidence.

Reference:

https://learn.microsoft.com/en-us/training/modules/analyze-text-with-text-analytics-service/3-get-started-azure

49) Correct answers are:

D. the Speech service.

E. the Translator service.

Out of the listed features, the two that can facilitate both text-to-text and speech-to-text translation across multiple languages in Azure AI Services are:

D. The Speech service: This service offers a wide range of functionalities related to speech processing, including:

Speech-to-text conversion: It can transcribe spoken audio into text format, supporting various languages.

Speech translation: It can translate the transcribed speech into another language in real-time or asynchronously.

E. The Translator service: This service focuses on text translation and provides capabilities for:

Text-to-text translation: It can translate text from one language to another, supporting a vast number of languages.

Can be integrated with the Speech service for a complete speech-to-text translation workflow.

Here's why the other options are not suitable for both text-to-text and speech-to-text translation:

A. Conversational Language Understanding: This feature focuses on understanding the intent and meaning behind conversations, not translation itself.

B. Key phrase extraction: This feature identifies important phrases within text, not performing translation across languages.

C. Language detection: While language detection helps identify the source language, it doesn't translate the content.

Azure AI Speech service can convert text into spoken audio for text-to-speech translation. Azure AI Translator service supports direct text-to-text translation in over 60 languages. Key phrase extraction, Conversational Language Understanding, and language detection are not utilized for language translation in the context of text-to-text and speech-to-text translation.

References:

https://learn.microsoft.com/en-us/training/modules/translate-text-with-translation-service/

https://learn.microsoft.com/en-us/azure/ai-services/translator/

50) Correct answers are:

C. key phrase extraction.

D. named entity recognition.

Two features of Azure AI Services that can identify problems from support question data and recognize individuals and products mentioned are:

C. Key phrase extraction: This service helps identify the main points and essential keywords within the support question text. By analyzing these key phrases, you can understand the core issue the user is facing.

D. Named entity recognition (NER): This service focuses on recognizing and classifying specific entities mentioned in the text. In this case, NER can identify:

People: Names of individuals mentioned in the support question, potentially customers or support staff.

Products: Names of specific products the user might be having problems with.

Here's why the other options are not as directly relevant to this specific task:

A. Azure AI Bot Service: While a Bot Service can be built to utilize key phrase extraction and NER, it's not directly a feature itself.

B. Conversational Language Understanding (CLU): CLU goes beyond just identifying keywords. It helps understand the intent behind the conversation, which might be helpful for broader analysis, but NER is more focused on recognizing specific entities like individuals and products.

E. Azure AI Speech service: This service is primarily for speech-to-text conversion. While the transcribed text could be analyzed with key phrase extraction and NER, it wouldn't directly address identifying problems and entities from written support questions.

Key phrase extraction is utilized to extract essential phrases that represent the primary concepts in a text. This feature enables a company to pinpoint the main discussion points in support question data and helps in identifying recurring issues. Named entity recognition categorizes entities in unstructured text, such as individuals, locations, organizations, and quantities. Azure AI Speech service, Conversational Language Understanding, and Azure AI Bot Service are not intended for identifying key phrases or entities.

References:

https://learn.microsoft.com/en-us/azure/search/cognitive-search-skill-keyphrases

https://learn.microsoft.com/en-us/training/modules/extract-insights-text-with-text-analytics-service/

https://learn.microsoft.com/en-us/training/modules/analyze-text-with-text-analytics-service/

51) The most suitable feature of Azure AI Services for Language to analyze written articles and extract information like individuals and locations for classification purposes is:

C. Named Entity Recognition (NER)

Here's why:

NER specializes in entity recognition: This feature is specifically designed to identify and classify named entities within text data. In this case, it can extract individuals (people's names) and locations from written articles.

Classification foundation: Extracted entities like individuals and locations can be valuable for categorizing articles based on the people or places they discuss. This forms the basis for tasks like news article categorization or research paper classification based on the entities mentioned.

Here's why the other options are not as suitable:

A. Azure AI Content Moderator: This service focuses on identifying potentially risky or inappropriate content, not specifically extracting entities for classification.

B. Key phrase extraction: While key phrase extraction can identify important words, it doesn't necessarily categorize them as specific entities like people or locations.

D. Personally Identifiable Information (PII) detection: While PII detection might identify some individuals, its focus is on privacy-related information, not all mentions of names in the context of classification.

Named entity recognition categorizes entities in unstructured text, including individuals, locations, organizations, and quantities, making it ideal for supporting the creation of an article recommendation system. In contrast, key phrase extraction, Content Moderator, and the PII feature are not tailored for entity recognition tasks in the context of building a recommender system.

References:

What is Named Entity Recognition (NER) in Azure AI Language?

Named Entity Recognition (NER) is one of the features offered by Azure AI Language, a collection of machine learning and AI algorithms in the cloud for developing intelligent applications that involve written language. The NER feature can identify and categorize entities in unstructured text. For example: people, places, organizations, and quantities. The prebuilt NER feature has a pre-set list of recognized entities. The custom NER feature allows you to train the model to recognize specialized entities specific to your use case.

Quickstarts are getting-started instructions to guide you through making requests to the service.

How-to guides contain instructions for using the service in more specific or customized ways.

The conceptual articles provide in-depth explanations of the service's functionality and features.

Note: Entity Resolution was upgraded to the Entity Metadata starting in API version 2023-04-15-preview. If you are calling the preview version of the API equal or newer than 2023-04-15-preview, please check out the Entity Metadata article to use the resolution feature.

https://learn.microsoft.com/en-us/azure/ai-services/language-service/named-entity-recognition/overview

https://learn.microsoft.com/en-us/training/modules/analyze-text-with-text-analytics-service/

52) Correct answers are:

B. ISO 6391 Code

C. Language Name

D. Score

The language detection feature of Azure AI Language service returns three outcomes to describe the detected language:

B. ISO 639-1 Code: This is the two-letter code assigned to the language according to the ISO 639-1 standard (e.g., "en" for English, "fr" for French).

C. Language Name: This is a human-readable name for the identified language (e.g., English, French, Spanish).

D. Score: This is a confidence score between 0 and 1 that reflects the model's certainty in the language detection. A score of 1 indicates the highest confidence level.

Here's why the other options are not returned by the language detection feature:

A. Bounding box coordinates: This is typically used in computer vision tasks to identify the location of objects in an image. Language detection deals with text data and doesn't involve spatial coordinates.

E. Wikipedia URL: While the service might be able to internally reference language information from Wikipedia, it wouldn't directly return a URL in the response.

The Language service of Azure's natural language processing (NLP) returns Language Name, ISO 6391 Code, and Score as three values. Azure AI Vision services in Azure return bounding box coordinates. Wikipedia URL is among the possible values returned by entity linking in entity recognition.

Reference:

https://learn.microsoft.com/en-us/training/modules/analyze-text-with-text-analytics-service/3-get-started-azure

53) Correct answer: A. entity recognition

Entity recognition incorporates entity linking, which provides links to external websites to clarify terms (entities) identified in a text. Key phrase extraction assesses the text of a document and determines its primary discussion points. Azure AI Language detection identifies the language used in the text. Sentiment analysis evaluates text and provides sentiment scores and labels for each sentence.

Reference:

https://learn.microsoft.com/en-us/training/modules/analyze-text-with-text-analytics-service/3-get-started-azure

54) Correct answer: D. text-to-text

The name "Translator" itself implies a focus on translating text from one language to another.

The documentation and marketing materials for Azure AI Translator emphasize its capabilities in translating written text across a vast number of languages.

While Azure AI Services offers other functionalities related to speech processing and conversion (text-to-speech and speech-to-text), these are separate services under the umbrella of Azure AI Services, not features of the Translator service itself.

The Azure AI Translator service facilitates text-to-text translation exclusively; it does not cater to speech-to-text, text-to-speech, or speech-to-speech translation.

Reference:

https://learn.microsoft.com/en-us/training/modules/translate-text-with-translation-service/2-get-started-azure

55) Correct answer: B. Azure AI Services

Azure AI Services offers direct access to both Azure AI Translator and Azure AI Speech services through a single endpoint and authentication key. Azure AI Language service provides access to the Azure AI Language service but not to Azure AI Translator and Azure AI Speech services. The Machine Learning service is utilized for designing, implementing, and deploying Machine Learning models. Azure AI Bot Service provides a framework for developing, publishing, and managing bots in Azure.

Reference:

https://learn.microsoft.com/en-us/training/modules/translate-text-with-translation-service/2-get-started-azure

56) Out of the listed machine learning models, the best choice for identifying the likelihood (numerical probability) of developing diabetes based on age and body fat percentage is:

C. Logistic regression

Here's why logistic regression is a good fit for this scenario:

Predicting probability of an event: Logistic regression excels at classification tasks where the goal is to predict the probability of an event occurring (in this case, developing diabetes). It analyzes the input data (age and body fat percentage) and outputs a value between 0 and 1, representing the likelihood of an individual falling into the category of "at risk" for diabetes.

Numerical output: Logistic regression provides a numerical output that directly translates to the probability you need.

Here's why the other options are not as suitable:

A. Hierarchical clustering: This is an unsupervised learning technique used to group data points based on similarities. It wouldn't directly predict probabilities for individual cases.

B. Linear regression: While linear regression can model relationships between numerical variables, it typically predicts continuous values, not probabilities between 0 and 1.

D. Multiple linear regression: This is an extension of linear regression that can handle multiple input variables (like age and body fat percentage in this case). However, it still predicts continuous values and wouldn't directly provide the probability of developing diabetes.

While multiple linear regression could be used as an initial step to understand the relationship between the factors, logistic regression is the preferred model for this specific task of predicting the probability of an event (diabetes) based on numerical input variables.

Multiple linear regression models the relationship between two or more features and a single label. Linear regression, on the other hand, utilizes a single feature. Logistic regression, a classification model, produces either a Boolean value or a categorical decision. Hierarchical clustering clusters data points with similar characteristics.

References:

https://learn.microsoft.com/en-us/training/modules/fundamentals-machine-learning/

https://learn.microsoft.com/en-us/training/modules/understand-classification-machine-learning/2-what-is-classification

57) Out of the given options, the machine learning algorithm that predicts a numerical label linked to an item based on the features of that item is:

C. Regression

Here's why regression is the most suitable choice:

Predicting continuous values: Regression algorithms are designed to model the relationship between features (independent variables) and a continuous numerical target variable (dependent variable). In this scenario, the features are the item's characteristics, and the target variable is the numerical label you want to predict. This label could be anything measurable, like a housing price based on various features (square footage, number of bedrooms, etc.) or the predicted customer rating for a product based on its features (reviews, brand, etc.).

Examples of regression tasks: Common regression tasks include:

Linear regression: Predicting a continuous value using a linear relationship between features and target variable.

Decision tree regression: Using decision trees to predict a continuous target variable.

Here's why the other options are not as relevant:

A. Classification: Classification algorithms categorize data points into predefined classes (e.g., spam or not spam email, cat or dog image). While the classes might have numerical representations, the goal is not to predict a continuous numerical value based on features.

B. Clustering: Clustering algorithms group similar data points together without any predefined labels. They wouldn't predict a specific numerical value for an individual item.

D. Unsupervised: Unsupervised learning refers to a category of machine learning where algorithms learn patterns from unlabeled data. While regression is a supervised learning technique, it's the specific algorithm within supervised learning that best suits the task of predicting a numerical label based on item features.

Regression algorithms are employed for predicting numerical values. Clustering algorithms group data points with similar characteristics. Classification algorithms predict the category to which an input value belongs. Unsupervised learning is a category of learning algorithms that encompasses clustering, but not regression or classification.

References:

https://learn.microsoft.com/en-us/training/modules/fundamentals-machine-learning/

https://learn.microsoft.com/en-us/training/modules/understand-classification-machine-learning/2-what-is-classification

https://learn.microsoft.com/en-us/training/modules/train-evaluate-cluster-models/2-what-is-clustering

58) Out of the listed options, the machine learning algorithm that determines the best method for dividing a dataset into groups without the need for training and validating label predictions is:

B. Clustering

Here's why clustering is the most suitable choice:

Unsupervised learning: Clustering algorithms fall under the category of unsupervised learning. This means they can learn patterns and relationships within data without the need for pre-labeled data. In supervised learning algorithms (like classification), the data is labeled beforehand, and the model learns to predict those labels for new data points.

Grouping similar data points: Clustering algorithms aim to identify groups (clusters) within the data where points within a cluster share similar characteristics. This can be helpful for tasks like segmenting customers based on their buying habits or grouping news articles based on their topics.

Here's why the other options are not as relevant:

A. Classification: Classification algorithms require labeled data for training and predicting predefined classes.

C. Regression: Regression algorithms also require labeled data to learn the relationship between features and a target variable.

D. Supervised: Supervised learning refers to the broader category where algorithms learn from labeled data. Clustering, on the other hand, is unsupervised learning.

A clustering algorithm is a form of unsupervised learning, grouping data points with similar characteristics without depending on training and validating label predictions. Supervised learning encompasses regression and classification but not clustering. Classification and regression algorithms are instances of supervised machine learning.

Reference:

https://learn.microsoft.com/en-us/training/modules/train-evaluate-cluster-models/2-what-is-clustering

59) The machine learning types the company should utilize to gauge user sentiment on social media regarding the new product launch campaign is:

A. Classification

Here's why classification is the best choice:

Sentiment analysis as classification: This task involves categorizing user responses into sentiment classes, typically positive, negative, or neutral. Classification algorithms excel at this type of problem where the goal is to assign data points (user responses) to predefined categories (sentiment classes).

Supervised learning approach: For sentiment analysis, supervised classification is often used. This means the model is trained on a dataset of labeled text data where each piece of text is already assigned a sentiment label (positive, negative, or neutral). By analyzing these labeled examples, the model learns to identify sentiment patterns and can then categorize new, unseen user responses.

Here's why the other options are not as suitable for this specific task:

B. Clustering: While clustering could be used to group similar user responses together, it wouldn't directly classify them into sentiment categories (positive, negative, neutral).

C. Data transformation: Data transformation is a preprocessing step that prepares data for machine learning algorithms. While it might be necessary before classification, it's not the specific machine learning technique used for sentiment analysis.

D. Regression: Regression algorithms are typically used for predicting continuous values, not discrete categories like sentiment classes (positive, negative, neutral).

Classification predicts data categories, determining which category or class an item belongs to. In this context, sentiment analysis can be performed on Twitter posts, assigning a numeric value to classify positive or negative sentiment. Clustering analyzes unlabeled data to identify similarities. Regression predicts numerical values. Data transformation is not a type of machine learning.

Reference:

https://learn.microsoft.com/en-us/training/modules/fundamentals-machine-learning/7-clustering

60) The machine learning types the healthcare organization should utilize to identify fracture types in new bone scans is:

A. Classification

Here's why classification is the best choice:

Identifying predefined categories: The task involves classifying new bone scans into predefined fracture types based on the existing dataset. Classification algorithms excel at this specific task where the goal is to categorize data points (new scans) into existing classes (fracture types).

Supervised learning approach: For this scenario, supervised classification is likely the most appropriate approach. The model would be trained on the existing dataset of labeled scans (each scan categorized by a specific fracture type). By learning from these labeled examples, the model can then analyze new, unseen scans and classify them into the most likely fracture type category.

Here's why the other options are not as suitable for this specific task:

B. Clustering: While clustering could potentially group similar fracture scans together, it wouldn't necessarily map those groups to the predefined fracture types the organization needs.

C. Featurization: Featurization is a data preprocessing step that involves extracting relevant features (characteristics) from the image data (bone scans) for use in the machine learning model. While crucial for preparing the data, it's not the specific machine learning technique used for classification.

D. Regression: Regression algorithms are typically used for predicting continuous values, not discrete categories like fracture types.

Classification predicts data categories, determining the category or class to which an item of data belongs. In this scenario, a machine learning model trained using classification with labeled data can be employed to ascertain the type of bone fracture in an unlabeled new scan. Featurization is not a type of machine learning. Regression predicts numerical values. Clustering analyzes unlabeled data to identify similarities.

Reference:

https://learn.microsoft.com/en-us/training/modules/fundamentals-machine-learning/7-clustering

Feel free to contact me on LinkedIn at "Georgio Daccache" for any assistance or questions. I'll be happy to help at any time.

Good Luck!

www.ingramcontent.com/pod-product-compliance
Lightning Source LLC
Chambersburg PA
CBHW060833220526
45466CB00003B/1087